Fine Silks and Oak Counters

Fine Silks and Oak Counters

Debenhams 1778-1978

Maurice Corina

Hutchinson Benham
London

Hutchinson Benham Limited
3 Fitzroy Square, London W1P 6JD

An imprint of the Hutchinson Group

London Melbourne Sydney Auckland
Wellington Johannesburg and agencies
throughout the world

First published 1978
© Debenhams Ltd 1978

Set in VIP Bembo by Input Typesetting Ltd, Wimbledon

Printed in Great Britain by the Anchor Press Ltd.
and bound by Wm Brendon & Son Ltd
both of Tiptree, Essex
ISBN 0 09 134910 9

Contents

Ginger and Pickles gave unlimited credit. Now the meaning of credit is this – when a customer buys a bar of soap, instead of the customer pulling out a purse and paying for it – she says she will pay another time.

And Pickles makes a low bow and says, 'With Pleasure, madam,' and it is written down in a book.

The customers come again and again, and buy quantities, in spite of being afraid of Ginger and Pickles.

But there is no money in what is called the 'till'.

But the sales were enormous, ten times as large as Tabitha Twitchit's.

'The Tale of Ginger and Pickles' by Beatrix Potter (Frederick Warne & Co., Ltd.)

To the loyal staff of Debenhams (1778 – 1978)

Frank Debenham's crest

Introduction

A Debenham coat of arms from a brass in Little Wenham Church

A Debenham coat of arms from a brass in Little Wenham Church

A Debenham coat of arms from a monument in Little Wenham Church

'LABORANTI BONA DEBENTUR'. This was the motto adopted by Frank Debenham when granted arms by the College of Heralds in 1902 after long searches of Parish and other records. Latin scholars may well smile at my somewhat flat translation: 'THE LABOURER DESERVES GOOD THINGS.' Clearly, the play of Latin with a draper's surname can be construed with more skill, yet the sentiment is an appropriate one.

When Frank Debenham set down a family motto, one of the most exclusive stores in London's West End linked a name familiar in shopkeeping for over 100 years with that of his mother, Caroline, sister of Clement Freebody. Within a few years, a new department store, the very best that architects and builders could design, reinforced the claims of Debenham & Freebody to offer shopping in the grandest manner, rivalling anything then available in London, Paris, or New York. Such a store was undoubtedly a showcase for the life and position enjoyed by the richest and most privileged classes. Yet it was through such stores that modern standards of taste, quality, and value were set when the inheritors of those great houses and enterprises assisted in the emancipation of future generations by offering competitive shopkeeping.

Excellence in shopkeeping, by definition, required the setting of standards. An assessment of the development of department stores, and of their place in social history, cannot ignore their early role of serving a minority of the population. Those master shopkeepers, whose service derived for themselves great reputations and traditions, were businessmen, not social reformers. Yet their part in social transformation deserves examination, for more than a few thought deeply and saw in retail trading a means for popular advancement.

At one time, staff at the original Marshall & Snelgrove store regularly received a small bulletin entitled 'Marshall's Broadcast'. One of its features was a regular quotation. An example, which might be set alongside Frank Debenham's motto, was 'There is nothing truly valuable which can be purchased without pains or labour.' The great writer Emile Zola put matters another way by describing department stores as contributing to the 'democratization of luxury'. Whatever my preference, both Zola's statement and the founding family's motto for Debenhams' personal philosophy say something significant about the development of a modern retailing group over a span of 200 years, ten reigns, and countless events of more interest to historians. Two centuries are but slivers of the realm's history, but they cover

9

the transformation of storekeeping from the contrasts of Georgian elegance and agrarian reform through the turbulence of industrial revolution to our modern democracy, within which people, both as producers and consumers, enjoy an unparallelled freedom of choice in the material things which master shopkeepers felt they always deserved.

The narrative which follows is no apologia for 'snobbery' in shopping. Indeed, I am grateful for the encouragement of Debenhams, in whose archives and among whose memories I have freely delved, to present a purely personal view of department stores and to brook no inhibition. Those who may search these pages for many names of long dead directors, managers, and staff will do so in vain, for what follows is no definitive history of Debenhams. Rather this is a study in shopping across twenty decades, to be offered hopefully as a contribution to our neglected literature on retailing. Any opinions on the exciting and potentially embarrassing developments, ranging from dramatic reforms in trading techniques to struggles in the stock markets, are mine alone.

Throughout my research, I have been constantly reminded that all our major retail enterprises have depended as much on their employees as their sense of direction. From humble scraps of paper, long forgotten memoranda, yellowing reports, faded photographs, letters, personal recollections, and archive material of all kinds there emerges a sense of common service to the customers. What divided one retailer from another were individual reputations derived from the collective efforts of employees.

I am indebted to many people whose help and recollections have guided me in the formative stages of this study. I know they will offer their understanding if all their time, words, and papers cannot be fully recorded in what follows, but their assistance has been invaluable and I can only offer my apology here for things missed, passed over, or inadequately expressed.

A particular debt exists to Mr Jack Mullins, a retired store director of Debenhams and a dedicated trader, without whose original single-handed research on the history of individual stores this book might not have appeared. I am grateful, too, for the assistance of Mr Angus Cater and Mrs Janet Kelley, whose patience with an outsider rummaging around Debenhams has been much appreciated. Their practical help has sustained the writer as much as Mozart and Vivaldi in the lonely hours of authorship.

MAURICE CORINA,
The Times, London April 1978

1 The art of Salesmanship

*Harvey Nichols' tailor-made suits and mantles are
made under the supervision of an expert Viennese
cutter and fitter. Perfect style and fit guaranteed.*

Advertisement, *The Times* 1914.

Few symbols of England's history can compare with her cathedral bells in
stirring our imagination. For those with time to pause, they echo down the
ages. Their chimes were heard on those chill dawns when medieval markets
opened.

The sounding of bells for Mass was often the signal for the local peasant
population to begin their trading in food, cloth, candles, and pottery. Equality of opportunity to engage in the babble of open bargaining was important.
Bells ringing across market squares usually prompted a mad scramble,
before the days of regulation, to see what some craftsman or smallholder had
to offer.

It is faint, perhaps, but the echo from the middle ages is not lost in the late
twentieth century as today's shoppers burst through the doorways of some
department store at opening time on the first day of a sales event. The urge
not to miss a bargain is the same, yet the essential difference is not so much in
the surroundings for buying and selling, rather a complete reversal of the
individual's whole attitude to life.

Markets were a principal means for a peasant population, lacking coin and
fair weights and measures, to ease their struggle for survival. The individual
was concerned with self-sufficiency. His dream was of a small herd, enough
grain, warm clothing, and freedom to gather wood and to hunt. They
needed markets to exchange their produce and to seek out essential items
beyond their own skills but made by local craftsmen and guildsmen. To
these markets, however, would come travelling chapmen, peddling goods as
middlemen.

So vital did markets become that regulations were necessary. Local
craftsmen developed rudimentary shops in town homes, joined by merchants
engaged in general trade. Mercers, haberdashers, grocers, and others have a
misty lineage. In markets, traders established regular 'pitches' and around
them arose generations of families who established workshops, ovens, and
services needed by farming communities. Early shopkeepers displayed
spices, silks, seed, furs, tools, weapons, honey, fabrics, and second-hand

clothes. London saw particular trades and skills move to specific areas. Poulterers, bakers, fishmongers, and dairymen set up stalls and small shops. Ships brought to great ports not just bounty but exotic foods, seeds, tea, tobacco – and people with great skills. Kings established great country fairs which attracted foreign merchants and stewards from great households with the means to buy Flemish cloth or precious stones and all manner of things beyond the resources of the locality.

The increased availability of coin and weights and measures, as England moved through her history to Elizabethan and Stuart times, promoted trade. Towns grew as centres for custom and trade as well as administration. Trades and crafts were nourished on the custom of the nobility and the gentry, the latter often offering sons in apprenticeship to early tradesmen and they in turn using family means to branch into ventures on their own account.

The patronage of ruling classes set new standards for workmanship while travelling courts set fashions and life styles. Merchants constantly sought to tempt the wealthy and landed with the finest clothes, the art of goldsmiths, and lacework. Victuallers prospered, and haberdashers and silk mercers, while the middlemen of early mercantile trade had obtained sufficient wealth by the 17th century for their houses of trade and showrooms to be commonplace in London and the market towns of the shires. The growth of towns required distributive systems to feed and to clothe the servant and other working classes. Cottage industries moved closer to cities to market their goods, increasingly bought by travelling middlemen. The City of London grew into a centre of trade and shopkeeping. Today, the names of its streets as much as the ceremonies of guilds and livery companies tell of their origins.

In the seventeenth century, haggling was still commonplace and the buyer was often at great risk from bad coin, or goods and foods of doubtful quality, workmanship, or freshness. People learned to deal with regular pitch-holders and shopkeepers. The buyer who did not beware was a fool, not an unfortunate deserving sympathy.

The devastation of the Great Fire of London led to the building of bigger and better premises for 'standing shop', as the phrase ran. Smaller traders fanned out to other areas. Rivalry between the City and other parts of London was intense. Feelings ran high when the Earl of Salisbury put up his New Exchange in the Strand to challenge the famous Royal Exchange by renting booths to retailers. Such shops were for people of rank and importance, whose alternatives for investment were limited to land and property and personal indulgence.

Early shopkeepers might have wealth and even certain influence, but they were subject to the whims and fancies of the capricious rich. Lawyers and the professional classes had their roots in great families. Those with court duties or pretensions to such circles aped the manners and customs of others. Daniel Defoe wrote in 1727 in *The Complete English Tradesmen*:

The retail tradesman must furnish himself with a competent stock of patience; I mean that patience which is needful to bear with all sorts of impertinence. A tradesman behind his counter must have no flesh and blood about him; no passions; no resentment.

The New Exchange, 1772
Radio Times Hulton
Picture Library

It was not easy for the eighteenth-century shopkeepers, who were often despised for their servility and lack of rank, and yet had to combine the maintenance of premises worthy of patronage by people of so-called quality with obtaining the value of goods that were often subject to bargaining. Scores were ruined and ended up in the debtors' gaol. Others traded with patience and success. One of their skills was to cultivate a reputation for style with the most valued customers of highest rank and position and treat others with a certain disdain. A trader would seek to impress with exclusivity of service and stock, knowing the pretensions of some to the possessions of others.

Shopkeeping became an art. Apprentices would learn not some craft, but the art of selling. Traders who employed, for high premiums, the sons of well born families or took them into eventual partnerships were better placed to deal with the man of fashion or the emerging carriage trade. Credit was afforded to certain great households to ensure constant patronage. Furnishing of stores in new styles enabled a shop to distinguish itself as suitable for a high class of person. New goods appeared, often of fine design, such as English chinaware for taking tea. The wives of the wealthy found in shopping a new means to pass leisure time and to express themselves within society. Many women were trained in certain fine arts and appreciated the silks and satins displayed by drapers.

Drapers were to set standards for selling and fair dealing which established new relationships between shopkeepers and customers. Fairness and honest dealing did not necessarily spring from those who served the poor, even if the sub-strata of retailing had its share of plain and fair dealers. Bad coin and cheating were everyday hazards for the unfortunates with small means, particularly in a growing place such as London. The indentures of children from good families ensured that some thought was given to training apprentices for more than putting up shutters or sweeping floors. Some were the equals of those they served in manner and perhaps background.

Nonetheless, drapers were tradesmen without defined positions in a society that began to value courtesy as well as the goods sold. Purveyors of fine cloth became absorbed not just in the skills of those who provided their stock but in their own skills of selection and then resale.

Defoe was not the only writer to seek art in selling. Robert Browning, who lived near the original premises from which Debenhams developed, found poetry in shops. Behind oak counters and amid fine silks and laces, many a draper sought words to express to his apprentices and their families the art he found in selling. Lawyers talk of a compelling argument and see art in advocacy; politicians produce fine literature and appreciate good Parliamentary draughtsmanship, but where is the art in buying and selling?

In the dusty and yellowing pages of the archives of Debenhams can be found a humble statement by one A. T. Quantrill, an employee of Marshall & Snelgrove, who saw art in service:

Art is striving for perfection. You may dream of the perfect Palace you will one day build, I may dream of the perfect sock suspender I will one day invent, but we are both artists in our way. We both affect the quality of the day and, to do this, is to feed the blood stream of the arts. The purchaser, either of a Palace or of a suspender,

keeps on expecting a better article for his money. He is right to do so, for otherwise there would be no progress. The artist and the manufacturer must produce it, the supplier must display it, and the salesman must explain and sell it.

It is the salesman's first duty to know what he is selling. He should also know what competition he has to face. Both his goods and his service will be compared with those offered elsewhere.

Let him examine his goods; if they are not the best obtainable at the price, there is no harm in telling his Supplier; if they are the best obtainable at the price, there is no harm in telling the Customer. Let him examine his service; Salesmanship is not merely the booking of orders. A machine can register orders quickly and efficiently, and needs only an occasional overhaul and a drop of oil; a Salesman needs three square meals and a new hat for his wife. He should see that he is worth the extra expense by knowing all there is to know about his goods and ensuring that this service is the best on the market. There is no task more degrading and more heartbreaking than trying to sell what you know to be an inferior article; on the other hand, it is most inspiring to know that you have a good article to sell and goodwill to sell it. Remember, SERVICE is your work; your work brings independence: independence is freedom. All whom we meet, our Employers, our Employees, our Customers, our Fellow Workers, offer opportunity for real SERVICE.

This former employee's words may be covered with dust, yet they express the classical views of the master shopkeepers who ran Britain's great department stores. In sharp contrast is an old handbook of rules prepared by Plummer Roddis, marked strictly private, which store assistants were expected to observe. They were in effect rules to promote the regularity, accuracy, and despatch of business to the satisfaction of all.

'No fines are imposed,' it declares, 'but the company will be unable to retain the services of any employee who is not prepared loyally to observe the same.'

There were nine golden rules, and upon them the reputation of Plummer Roddis was built. They were:

Rules

and suggestions

Hints to Assistants

Politeness **1**—Towards customers be invariably polite and attentive, whether they be agreeable or disagreeable, considerate or exacting, without regard to their station.

Conduct of Business **2**—In your first minute with a customer, you give her an impression not of yourself, **but of the house,** which is likely to determine—not whether she buys of you, but whether she becomes a buyer of the house or a talker against it. If you are indifferent she will detect it before you have spoken.

3—Never ask a customer what price she wants to pay before showing goods; show goods freely to all customers.

Attention **4**—Be cheerful and attentive to all, whether buyers or not. On no account must a customer be allowed to leave unserved until timely reference has been made to the Shopwalker.

Introduction **5**—Always try and sell something by introduction to every customer, but do it tactfully, or you might cause annoyance.

6—Sell nothing on a misunderstanding. The words 'Warranted' or 'Guaranteed' are better not used.

Promises **7**—Make no promise that you have any doubt about fulfilment of, and having made a promise, see that it is fulfilled.

8—Waste nothing, especially time.

Arrangement of Department **9**—In arranging your department, have this maxim ever before you: 'A place for everything, and everything in its place.'

In more modern times, sales assistants were sent to what were known as Draper's Summer Schools, to hear from earnest young members of the Incorporated Sales Managers Association the latest on theory and practice of retail salesmanship. In time there would come to shopkeeping management scientists, academics, staff given formal training, and even psychologists. Yet what impresses is the common sense of selling based on courtesy, honesty, cheerfulness, and fair dealing. It explains above all the nostalgia for the kind of service which gave department stores such well founded reputations.

This is not to minimize the severe restrictions on employees or to ignore the fact that customers regarded staff as mere servants, vulnerable to dismissal on complaint. Service with a smile remains as valid today, wherever an individual engaged in selling may be positioned within a store system. Pleasant manners and helpfulness can still make all the difference, even in the most scientifically managed chain store or supermarket. The fact that they are not to be found in all stores of every type has only increased the nostalgia of those who can remember the pleasure derived by the customer in a friendly and helpful store run on departmental, or other, principles. Yet several generations now know little of what it means as they bustle through impersonal chain stores and supermarkets, the latter unable to solve the problem of queuing (which, after the Second World War, self-service trading was intended to abolish) and bumping their trolleys at the check-out. As for manners, stores can only reflect their times, which include standards of behaviour derived from the people themselves.

Sifting, as the author has done, through old papers it is possible to find a lost romance about department stores: even in notes on lectures given by the London County Council Trade School for Girls on silks, or knitted goods. Consider these extracts:

The customer has as much right to talk as you. In fact, if you can get the customer to talk so much the better. You can find out easier exactly what is likely to please and what price, style, and colour is required.

Or,

What is appreciated is courtesy with politeness and above all you must give the customer the idea that you are prepared to 'camp out' all day to please if necessary – never appear in a hurry.

Excellence in service did not come to every shopkeeper who raised some grand building with lavish facilities. It came from the staff. Reputations which linger on came from thousands of loyal employees down the decades.

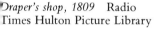
Draper's shop, 1809 Radio Times Hulton Picture Library

Their names are lost in the fading ink of counting house ledgers but they built great businesses and took pride in giving service. They understood that value was not just price, long before modern schools of economists invaded retailing. Even today the accountant, the High Priest of management decision taking, will admit that goodwill is a notional matter defying his attempts to give it accurate value. Goodwill can be built over a century or more, and lost in days.

This is not to say that selling and marketing goods cannot be enriched by the economist or accountant, so long as the impact of some theory or financial policy does not leave the customer out of their thinking. The department stores which suffer from an undeserved reputation for high prices may not have a corresponding reputation for personal service or a quality of merchandise to correct the impression. They fail. At the same time, the stores which cultivate an image as low-cost, highly competitive traders without understanding the meaning to customers of price and value can fall into difficulties, too.

The subjective value of money, or its utility, is not always the same as its monetary worth. The economic behaviour of men and women with the capacity to spend money still defies economic assumptions. The consumer is not a rational person, and price is but one attribute of an article and the inter-action of many factors on its way to the point of sale. Retailers are concerned with predicting behaviour and building reputations for their stores within which customers can exercise choice with a confidence appropriate to those reputations. Shoppers may not always appear rational, but they are not fools and frequently defy the whole chain of supply. There are many department store managers whose sheer experience and instinct can spot a winning line or predict a product failure without all the modern aids of experts who now pervade selling.

Is the age of scientific management and bulk purchasing, therefore, the destroyer of art in selling? The closing of many fine stores with all their traditions might seem to be vandalism, but, with the perspective of history, it is clear that some lost their souls long ago and society is well rid of them. They pretended to the traditions of others which survived and which understood the nature of social reform.

Imprudent management can take many forms. Exclusivity became confused in more than a few minds with social considerations rather than specialization and quality. This will emerge in our succeeding story of 200 years of shopkeeping. Equality of opportunity to buy good clothes and other things required stores to provide them at the right place, at the right time, and at the right values. To their credit, department stores generally understood their role as universal providers. They survived the onslaught of others who arrived to provide opportunities in competition with them, but only when they adapted to social requirements and the emancipation of each generation of shoppers. That qualification is important, for many stores failed and others, as we shall see, suffered their agonies from foolish insularity or losing their nerve in High Street warfare.

The British distribution system is among the finest in the world. Its efficiency indeed is not parallelled by equivalent performance in manufacturing.

Mergers and conglomeration have not stifled the growth by small companies into large-scale traders. Competition is fiercer than ever it was 100 years ago and, whatever the current consumer causes, the standards are higher and more diverse. Such is the pressure to win the consumer's favour that everyone has invaded everyone else's trade. It is evident to anyone who passes through the chain chemist, the variety store, the supermarket, or major newsagent. High finance and property development at enormous cost do not stifle competition: there is always the small firm growing at the expense of any large concern that takes itself for granted and neglects the most fundamental rule in retailing. That rule is that it is the performance of the individual store which matters, and woe betide the management which relaxes its attention to the point of sale.

Today, Britain is served by around 800 department stores which together handle around £2 000 000 000 in sales. Their share of national retail trade hovers around 6 per cent. It is still a mighty amount of business, always vulnerable to covetous competitors, many of whom are quietly departmentalizing their trade by diversification. The concept of departmental store trading is old, yet the most modern multiples and chains which now discover it to have advantages may rue the challenge. There is significance in the new association of Debenhams, for example, with supermarkets or specialist footwear chain stores.

The conventional boundaries of retailing are being blurred. What matters in the end is that it is the consumer who benefits from the twists and turns of competition. Whether trade shifts in or out of, or even around, town centres, the department stores still survive to this day. They have experienced the shifts and trends longer than any other form of shopkeeper, apart from the traders in the markets where it all began.

There can be no better advice to anyone in the higher echelons of retailing who feels he may have discovered the secret of successful shopkeeping than to take a walk in a street market, and go back there when all is quiet to listen to some nearby chiming bell. . . .

Dress shop, 1777   Radio Times Hulton Picture Library

2 Fine silks and Oak Counters

For Ready Money Only. . . .A large & elegant
assortment of cottage twills, stuffs,
bombazines, sarsnets, satins, millinery,
pelisses, & dresses.

From the Trade Card of Clark & Debenham's
Cavendish House, 1813.

Standing at the front door of his small shop at the end of a terraced property, William Franks would await the occasional arrival of an open horse-drawn carriage, from which a liveried driver would assist onto the walk-way some lady finely dressed in India muslin. Franks was a mere draper, whose stock of expensive cloth, ribbons, bonnets, gloves and fashionable parasols attracted a privileged clientèle to 44 Wigmore Street.

Gentle, sheltered women had begun to read new magazines for ladies and the growing pressures of Georgian fashion made them purchase and select items in person. They could not patronize the rough street markets of London, where household staffs were left to deal with provisions and visiting tradesmen. New shops which had begun to spring up around the London of George III, with its population of 700 000, offered comfortable places where rich and leisured women could attend to their most personal requirements, such as clothing and trimmings.

Formal dresses were often costumes ordered before adulthood and used rich brocades, pleated at the shoulders and fanning out from the waist over a cane frame. They were now being offered in a variety of new designs using silks, satins and delicate lace.

Franks would seat his visitors by an oak counter and display wares ranging from Brussels lace to Spitalfields silks. Personal attention was time-consuming and his customers were fussy and in no hurry, but the time spent with these ladies enabled him to cultivate customer loyalty which might produce useful recommendations in social circles.

The shop, trading as early as 1778, was close to dank pastureland owned by the Duke of Portland, which had been released for the building of town houses. Open fields were to become Portman, Cavendish, and Manchester Squares. From Duke Street to the village of Mary-le-Bone, masons and craftsmen worked urgently, transforming poor rural land into construction sites, even draining part of a reservoir at the end of Harley Street.

21

Above: *Map of old Marylebone*

Opposite: *Street plan of Marylebone*

Trade grew steadily as the new houses were occupied, often by rich families from distant counties seeking a base for participation in London society. Demand for drapery and related goods could flourish in such surroundings. The modest venture by which Franks and, later, a partner called Flint, secured his share of a rising trade did not, however, fully foreshadow the boom in fashion goods through the Regency. A high society draper such as Franks certainly could not have envisaged that new methods for producing some of the humbler cotton fabrics and linens he kept in stock were to transform England's history.

It was in the North, the Midlands, and to the East of London that the first impact of an industrial revolution, initially based on textiles, was understood. Traditional sources and centres of wealth and power were about to be overturned, separating England from her past. As historical fact, the yellowing rate books of Mary-le-Bone which record the existence in 1778 of Franks's shop are a mere trifle. Yet, through such traders, was provided the essential outlets for supplying manufactured fabrics, displacing the street markets and hawking on which cottage industry relied.

Travellers who brought in stocks of cloth from hand loom weavers in croft and cottage spoke of small factories which threatened the livelihoods of traditional spinsters and weavers.

The development of the flying shuttle by John Kay some 45 years before had increased the output of weavers while producing a problem of yarn shortages as everyone tried to keep pace. Now news was spreading of James Hargreaves's 16-spindle spinning jenny, while the fashion conscious were attracted to lightweight fabrics.

22

Technology had brought Arkwright's water frame, and Crompton patented his mule in 1779 to transform yarn production into a complexity of machinery and workmen. Factories were established, switching from water to steam power as men and capital began to exploit Watt's steam engine, patented in 1769.

Some idea of the impact can be derived from Customs statistics for raw cotton. In 1760, just over 3m lb were entered for home use. By 1778, the figure attained 50m lb, and, within seven years, Samuel Cartwright's power loom caused the disruption of hand-weaving and ensured mass use of cotton goods.

It is not fanciful, however, even against this background, to believe that Franks did not fully appreciate what was happening outside London. The reality of industrial production and the markets it would require were better understood by the father of the science of political economy, Adam Smith, who was 55 years old in 1778. He wrote:

To found a great Empire for the sole purpose of raising up a people of customers may at first sight appear fit only for a nation of shopkeepers. It is, however, a project altogether unfit for a nation of shopkeepers; but extremely fit for a nation that is governed by shopkeepers.

The Wigmore Street draper was not without his anxieties. These flowed from the mundane problems of maintaining sufficient stocks of any materials that took customers' fancy. The declaration of war with France posed problems for supplies of items imported from the Continent. Cotton was less of a worry to him, even though George III, who had been on the throne for 18 years, was engaged in the American rebellion. With the Declaration of Independence two years before and the adoption of the Stars and Stripes by the Continental Congress of 1777, it was, nonetheless, clear that sources of such commodities as cotton and tobacco from the colonial plantations could well be disrupted.

To understand the London in which Franks conducted his business it is helpful to identify 1778. Napoleon Bonaparte was nine years old, Jane Austen three, William Wordsworth eight, and Robert Owen and Sir Walter Scott but children of seven. London was served by flying coach services, and a 36-year-old architect called John Nash had begun to bring a new elegance to building. A younger Thomas Telford was still dreaming of great feats of engineering.

In the world of art, Gainsborough was at the peak of his painting. Sheridan was running Covent Garden and the actor David Garrick had only a year to live. That year Mozart was to write his concerto in C Major for flute and harp with orchestra. Adventurers were popular heroes. Bruce had discovered the source of the Blue Nile only eight years before, and in 1778 would come news of the death of Captain Cook across the oceans he and others were still charting.

Edmund Burke, then 49, was rising to great eminence in politics, yet to be challenged in intellectual circles by William Cobbett, then just 16, whose mind was awakening to the social plight of the mass of people. Adam Smith saw them as the market upon which extensive free trade might be built.

Churches rang with the newly written hymn 'Rock of Ages', whose author Augustus Toplady died that summer.

A new London club, Brooks's was formed by rich gentlemen from Almacks in 1778 and was the scene of huge gaming losses by many of the famous and successful figures in society, politics, and the developing world of commerce. This same year was born the most famous gamester and dandy of them all, George Bryan Brummell, dubbed 'Beau', whose contribution to fashion and Regency clothing is enshrined in many histories of the times. Sir Humphrey Davey, the chemist, perfected his mining safety lamp, and the rise of the coal-powered economy began.

England was a place where slaves were still being bought and sold. A High Court ruling protecting runaway slaves from return to their masters had brought misery rather than freedom, for in the St Giles district of London there was a colony of destitute blacks, known as Blackbirds, representing 3 per cent of the population of London.

Outside London, labour was migrating to Lancashire and Yorkshire, searching for work in the new cotton and woollen mills. Lancashire was becoming the most densely populated area outside London and streets of inferior cottages were sprouting in the shadow of the first factories.

To contrast Lancashire with Suffolk, five days' coach journey apart, is relevant to the small place of William Franks in retailing history. The former county was a place of raging social deprivation but exciting transition. The latter was a dreamy place of thatch and spire, immortalized by the painter John Constable who was but a babe of two in 1778. Both counties, however, touched the destiny of 44 Wigmore Street and other early haberdashers and drapers.

From the North came an endless flood of cheap cloth for universal purchase. New Regency fashions and styles combined airy light fabrics with expensive specialities, such as Honiton or Nottingham lace, Southampton hessian, or East Anglian silks. New wholesalers were appearing offering products at prices which enlarged their markets beyond the rich and privileged. Franks increasingly, from 1778, took care to widen his ranges of materials and finished goods.

In Suffolk and its environs, there was cause for concern. The first textile factories were undermining those cottagers whose crafts embraced a great wool trade. Norfolk and Suffolk had long been great suppliers of flax and later wool. Indeed, names such as Worstead, Kersey, Lavenham, Hadleigh and Lindsay are part of the early history of the wool and cotton trades. The cottages built by Flemish weavers were a reminder of even earlier associations with the clothing trades. Wool fairs were thronged with pack horses carrying local wares.

Among the place names of Suffolk is Debenham, derived from a great family and hard by Stowmarket. The Debenham family traces its ancestry to at least 1165 and one Lucas de Debenham. In 1778, however, in another village, Debden, there was a Robert Debenham, descendant of the line, who perpetuated it through his son, William, born in 1792. About this time, though the records are thin, Franks's original business in London passed into the control of a partnership between two men, Flint, whom Franks probably

The Naked Fashion, 1801

Muslin dress worn with a satin trimmed spencer and a satin hat, 1818

An early trade card showing the premises as they appeared in 1813

trained, and one Thomas Clark. Flint was not the only successor, for a J. Hartshorn, haberdasher, was granted the lease on Wigmore Street in 1786.

Flint was a noted name in London retailing. One of the first fixed-price, ready-money stores which had been established on London Bridge was Flint & Palmer, where Robert Owen, the philanthropic industrialist, worked as a child. Flint's of Wigmore Street had been a ready-money store, too, but its clientèle was very different from that patronizing the cheap Flint & Palmer haberdashery and drapery store until 10.30 pm at night. It can only be conjecture that the Flints were related in some way, but what matters is that Clark gained ownership of 44 Wigmore Street and secured its place in history.

Thomas Clark was a shrewd newcomer to retailing, who appreciated the goodwill built up by Franks and his successor Flint, but saw even greater potential. He improved the Wigmore Street shop by providing it with a full glass facade in which wares could be displayed to a passing population as well as to those who knew the premises by recommendation and past service.

Ambition and ideas, however, required capital and he was introduced in 1813 to William Debenham, by then 21 years old and offering £500 to invest in an equal partnership. An indenture signed on Christmas Day 1813 creating the partnership of Clark and Debenham marked the young Suffolk man's majority. Debenham brought to the partnership an experience in the wider world of textiles, for he had been apprenticed for some years to the relatively new wholesaling operations of the Nottingham hosiery manufacturer, I & R Morley (now owned by Courtaulds), which had embraced the machine age with great commercial skill.

It was normal for young men to be apprenticed by rich families to merchants and providers of commercial services. Indeed, while Debenham was learning the hosiery trade, another great name in textiles, George Courtauld Snr had emerged from his apprenticeship to a master Huguenot silk throwster in Spitalfields to run a silk throwing mill in Essex.

William Debenham, born in 1792, was a large-browed and, later in life, heavily-bearded man, with well shaped, alert and amusing eyes. He lived at Welbeck Street and later in St John's Wood with his wife Caroline (Freebody), daughter of Thomas Freebody, from Hurley in Berkshire.

Trained in the City and in Nottingham, he was alert to changing times. Nottingham had become a place of machinery and mass supply of hosiery. Pioneers failed where his first employer, Morleys, succeeded with steam power and patented equipment. It was a world apart, or so it seemed, from, say, the Spitalfields colony where Debenham sometimes went. There emigré French protestant silk weavers, whose products had commanded such high prices and earned their providers fine houses, were joined by weavers of cheaper cloth. Bethnal Green's meadows were covered by weavers' cottages and, as they felt the impact of northern machine-made products, whose prices were kept low by fixed wages as well as rising output, the East End area of London increasingly became a place of converting, finishing, garment-making and wholesaling, earning in later years the claim to be the centre of the 'rag trade'.

26

William Debenham

Just how the impact was felt and observed by Debenham and others is recorded by Charles Greville, the writer, in his diary in 1832 (*Memoirs*, Vol. 1, 1874):

A man came yesterday from Bethnal Green with an account of that district. They are all weavers, forming a kind of separate community. There they are born, there they live and die. They are for the most part out of employment and can get none; 1100 are crammed into the poor house, five or six in a bed, 6000 receive parochial relief. The district is in a complete state of insolvency and hopeless poverty.

The shop at 44 Wigmore Street

The new business of Clark & Debenham was founded at a time when travellers and producers sought out shopkeepers whose clients set the fashion. London's population had, by then, swollen to just over 1m, but purchasing power still rested with a minority. Bethnal Green's distress was repeated elsewhere. The poor and disadvantaged were objects for Christian sympathy, but trade had to flourish among those with spending power.

The area now known as London's West End was alive with the gaiety of the rich and successful. At the time of William Debenham's indenture into the partnership, London was the only major capital in Europe which Napoleon had not entered, even though the Emperor of France was only a few years away from defeat at Waterloo. Regency bucks dashed their horses down Piccadilly. The Prince of Wales gave grand balls at Carlton House and the Great White Bear Inn was thronged with bucks, actors, pamphleteers, and soldiers telling stories of Napoleon's waning influence.

Shopkeepers gravitated towards the West End to be closer to the centres of social activity. In 1812, George Swan was a typical newcomer, taking a haberdashery shop for £58 per year on the north side of Piccadilly in time for Nash's scheme to link Mary-le-Bone with the Liberty of Westminster by the building of Regent Street. Later came an expansion to other property by Mr Swan, who took a junior partner, Mr William Edgar, and immortalized their names in the heart of London.

Towards the end of George III's long reign, William Debenham and Thomas Clark had to take account of the dandyism, affected manners, and extravagant clothes of a peacock society peopled by such as 'Beau' Brummell, Mrs Fitzherbert, and Lady Hertford, the Prince Regent's favourite. Ladies had long been ornaments for men's admiration. Now men sought to be admired themselves, creating new fashions and demands on tailors and drapers. But the two men were wise enough to discern newer sources for business.

28

Tyburn Turnpike

Probably their most lucrative decision was to offer a family mourning service. High profits could be made by the developing trade in crimped and stiff black crapes, available both from Italy and from a number of English silk weaving concerns. The ritual of deep mourning was being popularized outside court circles. It had become fashionable for families with sufficient money and social pretensions to adopt mourning dress for up to a year or more after the death of a close relative. The etiquette of mourning was spread by magazines and, on occasions, extra sales came from the mourning of some public figure.

Clark & Debenham actively sought this business. The sale of silk mourning crape was very profitable and to ensure a continuing trade Debenham later even arranged complete funerals to secure the inevitable orders for dresses, cloaks, hats and household draperies. It is significant that the great business of Courtaulds was to be founded on the power weaving of this particular cloth, and Debenham bought stocks on keen terms but sold retail at rewarding prices, for the bereaved were little concerned with costs. The price-cutting common for linens and other cloth during the Napoleonic Wars was avoided by such skills. The enterprise was particularly well sited, close to a main route for carriages and coaches.

Oxford Street was one of the most imposing thoroughfares, though until 1825 it was called Tyburn Road by many people. The highway was a route to Oxford and became known as Uxbridge Road and Oxford Road. At the western end stood the notorious Tyburn gibbet where hangings of malefactors were commonplace until 1783.

The nearby Wigmore Street had been little more than a country lane. It took its name from Wigmore Castle in Herefordshire, one of the estates of the Harley family. Robert Harley, Earl of Oxford and of Mortimer, enjoyed the additional title of Lord Harley of Wigmore Castle. All these names were used to designate streets in the neighbourhood. At first, Wigmore Street (or

29

The Lord Mayor's Banqueting House, near Oxford Street

Wigmore Row as it was formerly known) extended only to the west side of Marylebone Lane, with houses on the south side only, and was the northern boundary of the original Oxford road. Once its buildings looked out across marsh and fields, almost as much frequented by footpads as Hyde Park, and one branch of the Tyburn River crept down towards it. Now the Oxford Street area had become something of a wonder after dark. It was lit by oil lamps and shops used new plate glass in panes of over a foot square to replace bottle glass, enabling the owners to give window displays. Shopkeepers often had backrooms where they lived, and they dressed in long wigs and silk waistcoats. The West End had clearly begun to rival the traditional centre of London retailing, the City. Cabinet-makers and carvers gravitated towards the area where the gentry came to see the latest and highest quality furniture commanding high prices.

Well-to-do people expected, and obtained, credit, or 'coming to terms' as the phrase ran. Sometimes accounts would not be settled for up to a year and many an outwardly successful shopkeeper experienced problems. Others, however, obtained, in their turn, long lines of credit from wholesalers. Cash business was always welcome, though shortages of gold and silver coin sometimes led to acceptance of a variety of foreign coins known to be worth their face value in metal. Private bank notes had come into use, too.

In the early eighteenth century, haggling was still common practice and customers had to be a match for clever retailers. Stock varied greatly in quality. People with money were expected to use their power of purchase in a way that made it clear to the shopkeeper that they knew what they wanted. Shopkeepers would lay emphasis on fashion to sell a product that might lack a traditional quality.

There was no halt in the advance of the machine age. The Napoleonic Wars demonstrated the virtue of mass production of cloth and garments, adding to the desperation of hand craftsmen in the woollen, cotton, and

30

knitting trades. Feelings ran so high that demonstrations became frequent, culminating in periodic destruction of property. On 10 January 1813, some fourteen people known to English history as Luddites were executed at York. Weavers' incomes continued to slump in dramatic fashion as the power looms and new spinning machines continued their relentless advance. Raw cotton imports, for example, had now soared to over 90m lb a year.

Outside London the restlessness of a growing population expressed itself in labour strikes and the formation of secret clubs and societies bent on reform or self help. The dawn of trade unionism and the Chartist movement had been blackened at the turn of the century by the *Combination Act* 1799, passed urgently through Parliament. The Act meant that any workman who combined with another to get an increase in wages or cut in hours could be brought before a local magistrate and given a term of imprisonment with hard labour. The first unions and friendly societies had to flourish in a twilight world.

The evident instability of society was regarded with increasing apprehension by many of those served by the young Debenham, yet the industrial revolution was producing newer breeds of people with money to spend in fine shops. These were mushrooming across the fashionable parts of London. Furriers such as Nicholay and Sneiders, the Haywards lace warehouse, and travel outfitters Carters, now established themselves in Oxford Street. In Piccadilly, Fortnum and Mason were over a century old when Clark & Debenham opened for trade. Peal & Co. the bootmakers, were neighbours. A Benjamin Harvey set up in Knightsbridge in 1813, three years after John Harris Heal chose the Rathbone district to the north for his venture.

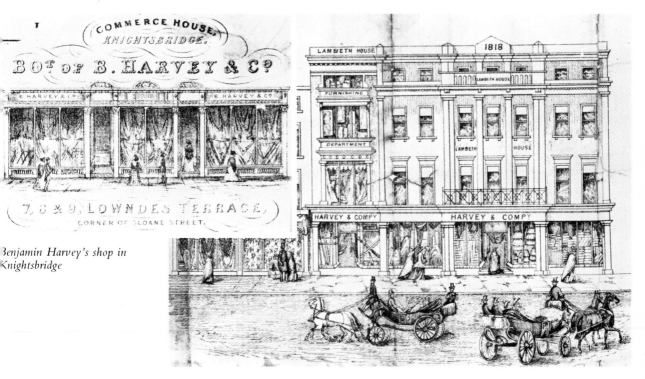

Benjamin Harvey's shop in Knightsbridge

The roots of London's great traders were being established. Ambitious tailors, drapers, and skinners joined the provisioners of foods and footwear in a scramble for sites that reflected their hopes of becoming suppliers of high renown. Many merchants bought themselves large houses to express their success, and those in trade and commerce, or mill owners from outside London, provided a new community in which ideas on trade and trends could be exchanged. This was a new aristocracy, less prone to the excesses of the blue blooded and reared on the virtues of church, diligence, and hard work.

One view of the period was expressed by John Bedford, a chairman of Debenhams, who compiled a brief history in 1966 of his group's development. He wrote:

To understand the relative slowness of the business to develop between 1778 and 1813, it is necessary to touch briefly on English history during these years. England had floundered from disaster to disaster in her relations with America until in 1775 the American War of Independence broke out, leading in due course to an American victory. The collapse of Lord North's administration in 1782 began a period of extreme instability which lasted until the emergence of William Pitt. Pitt set about reorganizing the finance of the country. His aim was to restore public confidence in the country's finances. He simplified customs duties and reduced them drastically on consumption goods to check the ravages caused by smuggling. Whenever he could, he abolished any measure which tended to check the flow of raw materials to British manufacturers or which impeded the export of finished articles. He then proceeded to negotiate a commercial treaty with France (1786) based on those same principles of free trade.

Pitt was not so successful in his handling of foreign affairs. His incapacity in this respect was most marked in his attitude to France. He distrusted the Revolution yet steadily reduced our naval armament and rejected all overtures of republican France for an alliance. In 1793 France declared war on Britain. This was to last on and off for over twenty years, culminating in victory at Waterloo, when Britain emerged the most powerful country in the world. But the war had aggravated the social disasters of rapid changes brought about by the beginnings of the industrial revolution. The defeat of France had opened the ports of the New World to commercial enterprise. Although in 1815 Great Britain seemed on the edge of bankruptcy and social revolution, the one hundred years peace that followed marked Britain's greatest advances in commercial power.

For his part, William Debenham, who had learned the hosiery trade, understood the importance of extending fashion to anyone with spending power. He knew something of the potential of the manufacturing processes and the cloth they could produce. He had an eye for laces and design, buying with great skill. Between 1813 and 1857, the business increased its capital fifty-fold from the original £1000. His acumen showed itself by early study of the potential of provincial shopkeeping.

Provincial shopkeeping was in its infancy. Town centres, however, usually revolved around markets and regular fairs where visiting salesmen moving from county to county would set up pitches. Tradesmen would provide services and take orders for later delivery. Customers were usually visiting the centres for specific purposes, and rarely made purchases on impulse. Budgets were tight, and even rich households would send out their stewards

Varwick House, Birmingham, 775

or other servants simply to obtain sufficient stocks of goods and foodstuffs. Self-sufficiency was their aim, not self-indulgence.

There were, however, a number of cities and towns where some fine shops had begun to appear, offering the fashionable items and wares to be found in London. Travel was still an uncomfortable affair, and it was to these centres that families would go to widen their social life. An aristocracy of money was becoming evident with the development of trade and commerce in the big regional conurbations outside London. They had begun to take houses and to spend seasons in places other than London. Cheltenham, Chester, and Harrogate, for example, offered entertainment and a chance to aspire to a higher social status by mixing with other monied people, who wanted shops to patronize and to confirm their importance in the community.

It had become the practice of more and more wealthy families to make half-yearly excursions to London's fashionable shops and even the cheaper City markets. Visitors often arrived with orders to supply their friends in the country, too. What was becoming clear was that, while this habit would continue to develop, there would be a growing need for good provincial stores to cater for trade throughout the year. Indeed, travelling pedlars were beginning to supply country stores with the latest goods, moving them by pack horses, and their trade grew to a point where London wholesalers began to complain of this method of distribution.

Travellers could leave factories and well sited warehouses and by-pass the London merchanting houses. The impact was greatest in the clothing trades. Cheaper hosiery, draperies and other products enabled more and more country shopkeepers to meet London's competition. Other travellers began supplying the new wage earners in the first factory towns, often using weekly credit systems of a rudimentary kind. The importance of pedlars became evident when in the 1780s the Government sought to make the practice illegal. Manufacturers of linen, cotton, and wool products protested vigorously.

33

William Debenham's wife was the sister of a man who had some experience in observing the craving for better shops outside London, Clement Freebody. For some time, after going into partnership with Thomas Clark, Debenham had observed the numbers of visitors from provincial centres, particularly the West Country, who expressed their pleasure at Clark & Debenham's stock and spoke wistfully of the lack of the same attention to fashion and variety outside London. In 1818, Debenham judged the time was ripe for an experiment, a real pioneering venture that now stands in the annals of retail history.

That year, along the promenade of Cheltenham, appeared a replica of the London store, proclaiming the best in draperies, silks, outfitting, millinery and gloves. The county sets of the West Country were soon flocking to the Cheltenham premises. Provincial shopkeeping, however, tended in general to develop by local people expanding their trade. A particularly fine example of county merchandising was Browns in Chester, opened as early as 1780. Clark & Debenham were also to extend their trials with branch shopkeeping to Harrogate.

Trade cards promised 'a large and elegant assortment of cottage twills, stuffs, bombazines, sarsenets, satins, millinery, pelisses and dresses'. A development was the extension of family mourning to include full funeral services, 'conducted in a most careful manner at moderate charges'.

CAVENDISH HOUSE
Promenade, Cheltenham:
No. 44 WIGMORE STREET, LONDON,
and HARROGATE, YORKSHIRE.

———————

DEBENHAM, POOLEY & SMITH

beg to announce their intention of OPENING their NEW and EXTENSIVE PREMISES on MONDAY NEXT, when they will offer for Sale a Stock unrivalled in extent, and selected with the greatest care from the British and Foreign Markets, consisting of every novelty in

SILKS, CACHMERES, SHAWLES, MANTELS, CLOAKS,
LACE and EMBROIDERY;
HOSIERY, FLANNELS and BLANKETS;
MOREEN, DAMASK, and CHINTZ FURNITURE;
SHEETINGS, DAMASK TABLECLOTHS,
and Linen Drapery of every description;
COBOURG AND ORLEANS CLOTHS;
A Large Lot of French Merinoes, Exceedingly Cheap;
READY-MADE LINEN, for Ladies and Gentlemen;
Baby Linen and Children's Dresses of every kind;

also

A CHOICE STOCK OF FURS
FAMILY MOURNING
FUNERALS conducted in the most careful manner, at moderate charges.

Above: *Trade card from Debenham Pooley & Smith, advertising the provincial stores*

Right: *Receipt from Debenham Pooley & Smith, 1839*

Management of the new provincial branches was vested in Clement Free-body, who was more successful in Cheltenham than Harrogate, where trading proved more difficult against some strong local competition. By 1837, Thomas Clark had decided to retire and Debenham took two faithful retainers, William M. Pooley and J. Smith into partnership – and until 1851 the business traded under the name Debenham, Pooley & Smith. This was necessary to bridge the time when William Debenham Jr and another son, Frank, could be trained to take over.

When that time came, with Pooley and Smith's retirement in 1851, he took William Junior into a new partnership which also included Freebody. The new trade name was to be Debenham, Son & Freebody, though the Cheltenham branch was to adopt the trading name, Cavendish House. Inspired by developments around Wigmore Street, such as Cavendish Square, named after the great Cavendish family, Clark & Debenham had first used the Cavendish House name.

These changes spanned a considerable period of social development and some particularly difficult years for trading. Napoleon was a costly adversary and the economic impact was to be felt for some time. The Prince of Wales first had assumed power as Regent with the lunacy of George III (during whose reign the population nearly doubled to 14m), and one year after the birth of Queen Victoria, in January 1820, he died. The accession of

The newly named Debenham & Freebody

An early photograph of the Debenhams ox-drawn delivery cart

William IV, who was to reign until 1837, saw the completion of more Nash buildings. Social unrest was expressed by the Manchester riots towards the end of Georgian times and complicated intellectual battles rooted in the counter arguments of revolutionary author Thomas Paine, whose *Age of Reason* and *The Rights of Man* were answers to Burke's reflection on the revolution in France and its implications for England.

There were moments of tranquillity amid social upheaval, such as the staging of the first Oxford versus Cambridge boat race, held at Henley, where Debenham & Freebody's Cavendish House clothes were well represented by a social class which had within itself intellectual divisions. New liberal thinkers were making an impact in politics, and the Houses of Parliament were destroyed by fire in 1834 just as Whigs and Tories divided into new political alliances. This period saw the world's first photograph, by Niepce, and the first public railway, Stockton to Darlington, upon which Stephenson drove his Rocket at 12 miles per hour and ensured the inevitable decline of canals.

Iron, coal, railways and mass production were the forces for wealth and reform in the cohesive Victorian years. New companies had developed, ushering in first the canals and then the railways, making a dramatic impact on communications and migration. The repeal of the *Bubble Act*, the abolition of slavery, and the historic *Reform Acts* preceded the death of William IV, by which time Peter Robinson had been established for four years in Oxford Street, and with its new department specializing in black crapes, began competing with Debenham's in the sale of mourning clothes.

Looking back, it is always difficult for the historian to evaluate particular events. History is never very tidy. For the shopkeeper, for example, the discovery by Faraday of electrical induction in 1834, or the premiership of Sir Robert Peel, who helped make London streets safer places for late-hour trading, had great significance.

36

Victorian shoppers in Regent Street   The Illustrated London News Picture Library

What was of particular interest was that Peel was the son of a manufacturer, a man of his age in terms of the phenomena of the industrial revolution and the need for more economic regulation. The introduction of income tax by Pitt had been a straw in the wind. Landed interests had dominated the eighteenth century Parliaments, but a newer breed of rich merchants and manufacturers was not fully enfranchised and it was evident that parliamentary representation was hopelessly at odds with an increasingly industrialized population. The French revolution in 1789 had prompted a reaction against property and privilege. Liberal ideas flowing from Chatham, Pitt and Fox coincided with a growth of non-conformity.

It was the enfranchisement of the middle classes under the *Reform Acts* that ensured the glory of Victoria's reign, which was one of the great ages for shopkeepers.

Trade had been made respectable under William IV and now votes brought a solid place in the pattern of power in Britain. Property development and railways meant Britain's past could be put behind her and although there was still desperate poverty, the means for spreading wealth now existed.

Many people born in the ages of Georgian and Regency elegance had begun to be displaced by people who understood the significance of canals on trade, coal mining, and great feats of engineering. Ironmasters, potters and others embraced mass manufacture, while flying coaches drove swiftly on the new roads built by Telford and surfaced by Macadam. The new heroes would be the great engineers, taking their place alongside the soldiers and statesmen, much admired in middle-class trading circles.

The future could be seen taking shape in London. The great docks were being expanded. Steam coaches began to appear and public transport became easy as rival operators fought for custom. William Debenham on his journey to the City to see his banker would be passed, for example, by a three-horse vehicle pulling a public carriage with inward facing seats. Many people abandoned the hansom cab for the cheap public carriages.

Forge hammers and engines were appearing outside London. Iron-framed buildings, first used for factories, offered a new potential. Retailers could not be isolated from changing times.

Increasingly, the time of William Debenham was taken up with controlling his buying and financing. His policy was to buy textiles and all related items and to strive for a family trade that spanned requirements from birth to death. He bought and supplied baby linen, children's dresses of every kind. For the home he now offered flannels, blankets, sheetings, damask table-cloths, and linen drapery of every description.

The practice of bargaining began to die away. More traders used price tickets, appreciating the merits of fixing prices to obtain a planned profit margin while developing a trade with lower income groups. A Report of the Select Committee on Manufactures and Trade commented in 1833: 'It is not a practice that would be resorted to by those who seek their custom from the higher class of community.'

It is necessary to understand that shops opened for long hours and, until the arrival of gas light, the conditions for selling after dark were not ideal. Apprentices were up in the early hours cleaning and preparing shops, sometimes sleeping on the premises, even under counters. Traders had to reflect social requirements. Even at the highest end of income scales there was much sewing and embroidery and drapers would supply the cloth and materials. Worth noting is the fact that among the earliest multiple retailers were the manufacturers of home sewing machines.

Receipt from Swan & Edgar,
1826

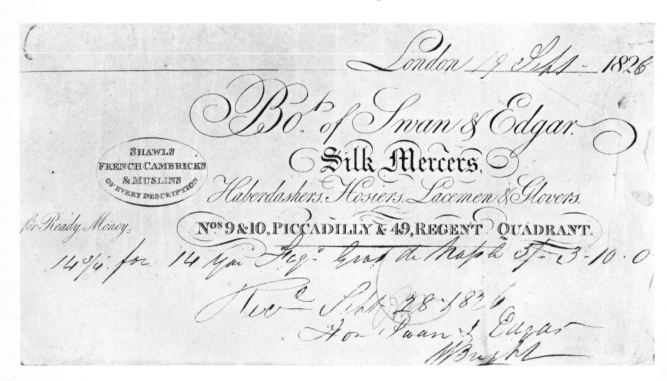

Debenham took care to retain a style and service appropriate to the original class of customer, but cannily stocked machine-made linens that interested a wider range of people. Silks, furs, cashmeres, shawls, mantles and cloaks were still specialities as were lace and embroidery. The problem was to retain a reputation for any speciality and this was met by the creation of departments for particular lines.

The concept of departmental store trading was clearly in its infancy. It usually takes young men to shrug off tradition and past rubric, and so it was with the early Debenham business as William's sons came into the business, learning their trade the hard way but quietly reflecting on the changes they might make in due time.

Marshall & Snelgrove

3 Victorian Shopkeeping

The Princess Victoria had set her heart on buying a doll she had seen in a shop window. But her mother, the Duchess of Kent, did not let her buy it until her next allowance of pocket money enabled her to do so. At last the day came, when she hurried to the shop, paid over the six bright shillings, and got the long coveted doll. On coming out of the shop with her treasure in her arms the young Princess encountered a wretchedly miserable tramp, who plucked up his courage and asked for help. The Princess Victoria hesitated a moment; then, realising that she no longer had any money left for the man, she returned to the shopkeeper and gave him back the doll. He gave her the six shillings again, promising to keep the doll for a few days. The little lady hurried out of the shop and thrust the whole of the money into the hand of the poor beggar, who was astounded at his good fortune.

The Marquis of Lorne, later Duke of
Argyll, *V.R.I, Her Life And Empire*, 1901.

After the coronation of the young Queen supported by the emerging middle class, most individual retail traders appeared slow to appreciate the expansion of purchasing power of any but their own or superior income groups. It was a mistake that delayed the alleviation of suffering among the poor and, indeed, prolonged exploitation when a new breed of shopkeepers could have afforded opportunities for fair dealing in pleasant and convenient premises to a wider section of the community.

Development of new stores was slow in the first part of Victoria's reign lasting from 1837 to the turn of her century, notwithstanding the opening of a small number of large premises in county towns, seaside resorts, or even places such as Newcastle where Bainbridges pioneered a form of departmental trading that attracted much interest. The establishment of Marshall & Wilson (later the renowned Marshall & Snelgrove) in Vere Street, London, in the very year of accession might with benefit of hindsight seem a portent, yet at the time it could only have been regarded as confirmation of the pre-eminence of London and its preoccupation with higher income groups. The opening of Harrods as an exclusive food store in the comfortable surroundings of Knightsbridge was an event far removed from the harsh realities faced by the mass of working classes.

41

Today, the remaining facades of nineteenth-century shop building, wit
their illuminated clocks and soaring windows, and premises with wide er
rance halls, mahogany and plasterwork, are a reminder of the developmer
in Victoria's later years. Early premises were torn down and replaced b
emporia and retail palaces, which dominated towns and created High Stree
to which other traders were drawn as though by magnets. Small trade
would huddle in the shadow of such stores when they began to promor
shopkeeping for the masses.

Victoria began her long reign with most of her subjects struggling o
pitifully low weekly wages, yet aspiring to become an affluent lower middl
class. In Merthyr Tydfil, which was coping with the coal revolution, ther
was no draper. The poor struggled against debt and clever tradesmen. Th
'Tommy' shop, the pawn broker, and new tally men were part of a reta
trader's substratum far from Wigmore Street. Second-hand clothing, adul
erated food (there had to be an Act of Parliament in 1860 to stop that) and th
absence of the services enjoyed by higher income groups added up to
twilight world. In contrast to brewers, retailers often avoided trading i
many areas. Their absence was unfortunate in the great spinning and weav
ing towns created by the industrial revolution. It prompted mill and min
owners and other employers to open truck shops, leading to the degradin
sight of women presenting pay records (Tommy books or tickets) to get th
groceries and other essentials.

The young Disraeli, who entered Parliament in the year Marshall & Sne
grove was founded, was to understand the social deprivation better tha
most, writing of the problem of vanishing wages that did not buy an impro
ving standard of living. Curiously, it was out of a desire for political expres
sion and reforms that a movement much concerned with shopkeeping fo
the masses had sprung to remedy part of this problem. The creation of reta
cooperative societies, run by amateurs, often with deep Christian beliefs an
driving liberal ideas, became inevitable, given the social deprivation of s
many people. By 1867, there were 577 cooperative societies, trading i
voluntary competition with private enterprise and marching on to become
giant in retailing for many decades. They paid back trading surpluses b
dividends to members, and ensured that competition would extend to prices

The idea of popular shopkeeping was nonetheless slow to take root whe
so many retailers were concerned with their individual businesses and it too
a special foresight to see any future in branch trading as known in presen
times. There were a few people with such intuition. Thomas Lipton built
fortune from a pantry shop opened in Glasgow in 1872. Before the end of th
century he had 245, serving cheap food in Lipton's Markets, and handle
one-tenth of the national tea trade alone. In other trades, London was i
danger of losing its innovative role in retailing. Lewis's in Liverpool an
Kendal Milne in Manchester took initiatives in departmentalized tradin
which would spur London from its slow start to Victorian development.

When the race began, the impact was felt after the death of Willian
Debenham Senior freed his sons and Clement Freebody to take on, in
flurry of extensions, conversions and new buildings, the newcomers o
Whiteleys ('Everything from a Pin to An Elephant'), Harvey Nichols, Mar

shall & Snelgrove, Peter Robinson, Maples, and others. London's burgeoning class of white-collar workers and the new suburban dwellers were to be wooed by a range of central stores the like of which not even the young Debenhams, with their bright ideas, could have foreseen.

Spending power would be tapped mainly by new entrants to retailing. Chains for the selling of specialist items such as footwear (Lilley & Skinner), newspapers (W. H. Smith), hardware, tobacco, even ready-made suits would soon spring up.

Chartist riots in Birmingham in 1839, a year before the penny post began, and great events, such as the Irish Famine, repeal of the Corn Laws (1846) and the *Ten Hours Factory Bill (1847)* provide some idea of the times before Debenham, Son & Freebody was created in 1851. William Debenham Senior lived another twelve years, by which time John Lewis had set up in Oxford Street, and Derry & Toms had chosen Kensington High Street to open its doors for the first time. During this time came the *Limited Liability Act* and Bon Marché was established in Paris, claiming to be the world's first truly departmentalized store for goods of all kinds.

43

Frank Debenham

Debenham Senior lived, however, to see considerable extensions to h original London store at 44 (later renumbered 23–27) Wigmore Street, swa lowing No. 42 and spreading to 2/3 Welbeck Street. It was a useful additio to Victoria and Albert's London, but one which expressed Debenham diligence towards the end of his fifty years of profitable trading, rather than new soaring ambition.

Six years after the founder's death, his brother-in-law, Clement Freebod died too, leaving the London and Cheltenham based businesses in the hand of William Junior and his younger brother, Frank Debenham. Frank was t prove a man of radical new ideas. It was not uncommon for smaller retaile to go to larger stores to buy stock in bulk, and the requests for supplies o special terms had grown markedly. There was clearly a demand for whole saling of goods bought with skill and an eye to fashion.

Born on 3 November 1837, Frank Debenham, who was married at 26 t Emma Folkard Ridley, was the fifth and youngest of the old Willia Debenham's children. He and his wife took a house in Fitzjohns Avenu Hampstead. Frank was a fine figure, partial to broad-lapelled frock coats an waxing his moustache. He joined the Reform, Devonshire, and Nationa Liberal Clubs over the years and became part of the establishment, serving a magistrate. The young man was always proud of his ancestry and spe much time in later years researching the family history and, with the help the College of Heralds, obtaining a new grant of arms.

His elder brother, William Debenham Junior born in 1824, had no chil dren from his marriage. When he died at The Priory, Tunbridge Wells, was Frank who ensured the continuity of the business dynasty through very able child, Ernest Ridley Debenham, born to Frank and Emma in 1865

Frank's horizons had been widened by residence and travel on the Conti nent before he entered the business as an apprentice in about 1857. He bega the wholesale trading. His ambition was that the firm should supply not onl the consumer, but the retailer and the dressmaker. Furthermore, he initiate the unheard-of practice of supplying small quantities of materials to dress makers who until then had been compelled to buy at least half a piec (anything from fifteen to twenty yards) or pay the retail price. He als offered them matching facilities and loaned them lengths of cloth to show t their customers. As a consequence London dressmakers flocked t Debenhams who were known to stock a wide range of the latest and bes goods.

Always determined to buy at the source, he and his buyers every yea travelled abroad. The results of visits to Brussels, Malines and Valencienne brought the firm a reputation for its laces. The extension of this policy t other lines soon made the business equally famous for silks. Long befor 1870 the firm had been regularly buying silks at Lyons, St Etienne and othe places in France and Italy, and later permanently established its own buyin houses in these centres.

The story is told that when the Franco-Prussian War broke out Debenham representative hurried to France laden with bags of sovereign with instructions to buy all the silks he could. This was matched by anothe enterprising transaction which helped to establish Debenhams as

Debenham & Freebody – Brussels
Warehouse

wholesaler. It was the purchase of the entire output of a large manufacturer in Brussels of gloves of excellent quality. They were advertised to the public at 2/11d a pair and, at the same time, sold by the dozen to retailers at wholesale prices. Thereafter the firm specialized in Brussels and French kid gloves and by bold buying maintained a lead in this particular line for many years.

Another important factor in the rapid growth of Debenhams was the adaptation of knitting machines to the production of garments other than stockings and gloves. For some time experiments had been made by the manufacturers of Leicester and Nottingham and at last they perfected machinery by which woollen underwear could be turned out in large quantities. Alert for novelties, Debenhams seized the opportunity to produce or get produced, under their direction, a new kind of garment. One example was called the Jersey, adapted from the familiar one-piece woollen trunk with sleeves that had first been in use (knitted by hand of course) among the peasants of the island whose name it bears. As soon as the machine-knitted jersey became a practicable merchandising proposition, Debenhams ordered in huge quantities.

A special department was then created. Originally the wholesale section of the business consisted of only five other departments, costumes, silks, gloves, ribbons and tulles, and the wholesale and retail trade drew from a common stock. The growth of the wholesale business made it necessary to separate the two businesses and to seek means of enlarging the premises for the expanding business.

The first of a number of acquisitions would follow, that of Foster's of Wigmore Street, manufacturers and retailers of artificial flowers and feathers. A wholesale millinery department was instituted and it became so successful that a factory had to be opened at Luton.

45

Other important purchases around this time were:

Laugher & Cousins, Oxford Street	Retailers of laces, lingerie and fancy goods
Christian & Adams, Cavendish Street	Retailers of lingerie
Nicholay & Co, Oxford Street	Furriers to Queen Victoria
Wright & Green	Costume and Mantle Manufacturers
Waywards	Leading House in London for real lace
Capper's of Gracechurch Street	Established for over a century supplying linen to Queen Victoria
Blunden & Banyard	Juvenile Outfitters
Helbronner's of Wigmore Street	Ecclesiastical, Heraldic and Domestic Embroiders, holding Royal Appointment

Frank Debenham took on the task of developing further the wholesaling department, starting with fabrics and laces carrying the Debenham & Freebody reputation.

Success was very soon to be evident in a surge of new business, which required bolder buying. Frank's ambitions were to be further realized by the rapid development of the export trade which grew so large that offices had to

Debenham & Freebody – the lace department

Debenham & Freebody – Paris warehouse

be opened in Paris, Brussels, Copenhagen, The Hague, New York, Melbourne, Sydney, Johannesburg, Montreal, Toronto, Buenos Aires, Valparaiso, Montevideo and even China.

Wholesaling and exporting on the strength of a name created in fashionable London circles was turning the business away from its origins in conventional retailing to the role of middlemen. These activities were profitable and raised turnover on a scale which required, in the interest of balance, some impressive development in shopkeeping operations.

However, this was to be delayed for many years, though the rebuilding of Wigmore Street in 1883 kept the presence in retailing very much alive. Between 1870 and 1900, Frank and William were to take over a succession of businesses.

An army of packers, despatchers, and ancillary staff were recruited to cope with the wholesaling, which included even flowers. Great premises and counting houses would be opened in Mill Hill Place and Welbeck Street to send out draperies, dresses, feathers, ornaments, millinery and haberdashery. A huge City warehouse, destroyed in the Second World War, was established in St Paul's Churchyard. Fleets of pedal and horsedrawn vehicles serviced the wholesaling depots, within which teams of wing-collared mustachioed men made up orders and poured over huge ledgers chronicling the burgeoning sales of catalogued goods. Customers could visit deep-carpeted and vast wholesale gown departments to inspect models showing the latest offerings. Top-hatted representatives from other big stores such as Harrods, Barkers, Selfridges and Bentalls began to buy from Debenham & Freebody's wholesale departments. Making-up operations followed, with women turning out shirts and other garments to keep pace with demand. Printing shops were organized and overseas warehouses were built on a grand scale to reflect the expansive development into wholesaling.

47

Debenham & Freebody West End Warehouse

The Town Travellers' Room

The Entering Room

It is a curious fact that Debenham & Freebody appeared to be surrendering any pretensions in the battle for retail eminence, preferring to supply other stores. Rather than weakening its future in pure shopkeeping, the resources were being generated for a counter-attack on the Victorian newcomers to London and the developing department stores.

Through the momentous years of the American civil war, the enfranchisement of Britain's urban working class, the *Education Act*, the legalization of trade unions and the introduction of electric lighting, it seemed that Debenhams had opted out of the movement towards shopkeeping for a

Delivery Vehicles

The Shirt Room

wider community, which was being steadily liberated. Through the Crimean and Boer Wars, Royal Jubilees and Gladstonean reform, it was others who embraced the great Victorian age of popular shopkeeping. The wealth of the nation was evident, yet Debenham & Freebody seemed content to look to expanding markets abroad and act as a wholesaler.

There were, by 1870, around 3m people crowded into London. This was the centre of world power and the world's largest city. Between 1815 and 1876 Britain's industrial expansion averaged 3 to 4 per cent per year – twice the rate in the eighteenth century. Indeed by 1860, the nation had achieved

TO AMERICAN LADIES & GENTLEMEN.

WHOLESALE   (Established 6o Years.)   AND RETAIL.

SWAN & EDGAR,
39 TO 53, REGENT STREET,
9 TO 11, PICCADILLY, LONDON,
Offer for inspection their Select and Varied Stock unsurpassed by
any in the United Kingdom.
All Goods marked at the lowest Cash Prices.
NOTED FOR
BONNET'S BLACK SILKS,   BALBRIGGAN HOSIERY,
IRISH POPLINS,   SCOTCH PLAIDS,
WATERPROOF MANTLES, RUSSIAN SABLES,
INDIAN SHAWLS IMPORTED DIRECT.
Departments—

SILKS,	COSTUMES,	DRAPERY,
SHAWLS,	MANTLES,	HOSIERY,
FURS,	DRESS MATERIALS,	HABERDASHERY,
LACE,	GLOVES,	RIBBONS,
OUTFITTING,	MILLINERY,	MOURNING.

DRESSES, COSTUMES, AND MANTLES MADE TO ORDER ON THE
PREMISES AT THE SHORTEST NOTICE.
Patterns Free.

*Swan & Edgar's advertisement to Ame­
can ladies and gentlemen, 1873*

complete industrial supremacy in world markets, supplying around half th
world's coal and manufactures. Britain's export trade was more than France
Germany, Italy and the US combined.

With hindsight it can be appreciated that the Debenham partnership a
wholesalers was giving valuable insights into competitors' buying policies.
let others do the High Street selling, while the brothers learnt much abou
really large-scale buying and supplying. Frank Debenham was to become
driving force and, when William Junior retired in 1892 after 40 years, it wa
Frank's son, Ernest, who entered into the succeeding family partnership
They changed the name in 1900 to Debenham & Co. and within four year
converted the enterprise into a private limited company.

Ernest was to repeat past experience by bringing in another young man'
ideas. He was quick to challenge the neglect of retailing. The relentles
growth of others was evident and there was a need to protect the Debenhar
name which had originally been built on high quality retailing over mor
than 100 years.

There was no doubt about the ability of Ernest, a slim, good-lookin;
27-year-old arts scholar fresh out of Trinity College, Cambridge. Ernest wa
an intellectual. He had eight children, one of whom, Piers K. Debenhar
(born in 1904) in due course entered the family concern.

With pointed ears and the family's fine eyes, Ernest adopted the fashion
able middle hair parting, and cultivated a shaggy, drooping moustache. H
later built a fine mansion in Addison Road, Kensington, with a mosaic dom
designed by his friend, Halsey Ricardo. (The house was used in 1969 by th
film director, Joseph Losey, in his film *Secret Ceremony*, and was later con
verted as a refuge for mentally handicapped people.)

Ernest's ambitions on accession to the partnership developed toward
retailing. Cambridge University had given him many friends and a wide
circle of people was open to him in assessing future trends.

Ernest Ridley Debenham

Early Victorian mantles from Swan & Edgar

Wholesaling was undoubtedly good business. Bulk supply of frocks meant the sale of huge amounts of material. In 1898, for example, one frock could contain fourteen to sixteen yards of silk and about twelve yards of taffeta for lining.

One afternoon dress would comprise:

Requirements for an afternoon dress in 1897.

15 yards of wide silk
 5 yards of skirt lining
 3 yards of horsehair cloth to stiffen the skirt
 4 yards of silk for a dust ruffle
 5 yards of velveteen skirt binding
24 inches of skirt belting
24 inches of waist belting (this allowed two inches to turn under)

1½ yards of sleeve lining
 1 yard of crinoline to stiffen the skirt
12 inches of buckram for the collar stiffening
 4 dozen fancy buttons
 1 card of large hooks and eyes
 2 cards of medium hooks and eyes
 1 card of invisible hooks and eyes

 5 spools of silk thread
 3 spools of cotton thread
 4 spools of buttonhole twist
2½ yards of featherbone for the waist
 1 yard of small boning for the collar
 1 bolt of seam lining

The Coplye Herald

51

In bulk, orders for these lines were lucrative and gave Debenhams buying power with suppliers that it could never achieve with one or two stores. And, for Ernest, there was always a nagging anxiety that expertise in retailing should be preserved. The Debenham name would need to be kept before the public and some grand scheme to refurbish retailing operations might allay his anxieties as heir to what had become an export-orientated merchanting business.

The success of stores such as Marshall & Snelgrove and Harvey Nichols had to be matched before it was too late. The former was gaining a big reputation with the carriage trade, and Victorians had begun to flock to this and other stores, offering wider ranges of goods and the latest in shop design, comforts, delivery and discreet credit accounting. In provincial towns and cities family firms had begun to emulate the big London stores, often offering better profits and being less constrained about encouraging what had once been disparagingly called the 'popular' trade, as if it was unworthy of a retailer of great reputation in elevated London circles. Such stores transformed many town centres and created distinct identities, reflecting regional tastes in goods of all kinds. Some were purpose-built with the help of Victorian developers, others just grew by swallowing neighbouring properties as their business expanded.

Many of these very individual stores were destined to fall into other hands and Debenhams & Co. were among the surviving giants, who eventually took them over, sometimes retaining their identity or submerging them to some central plan for reform.

By the late nineteenth century, provincial towns had experienced a boom in central shopkeeping. For example, drapers and house furnishers, Footman Pretty & Co., Ipswich, Harwich and Woodbridge (1815) built a splendid palace, Waterloo House in Ipswich. Not far away, in Norwich, the Curl brothers (in 1860) operated as retailers and wholesalers from constantly expanding premises, including a local inn. Letters show Curls was the subject of rivals' complaints about keen prices for such goods as worsted cloth. In 1889, a Cornishman trained in Bristol, J. R. Pope, set up Bon Marché Drapery Co., in Gloucester, where he became High Sheriff. The original premises were superseded by vast four-floor premises. In Hull, Thornton-Varley had been in operation since 1870.

In Southampton Edwin Jones (in 1860) began trading in East Street and grew to magnificent size. Worthing reared the business of John Hubbard (1870). Plymouth fostered Joseph Spooner's venture into drapery and furnishing (1858). Thomas Jones established a mixed food, tobacco and drapery business in Bristol (1843). London's suburbia spawned Sopers of Harrow, Staddons of Plaistow and, further afield, Kennards of Croydon. A Preston-on-Stow farmer, J. C. Smith, set up in Stratford–on–Avon (1870).

Retail historians are rare and, while few in number, they have argued continually over the origins of these and many other department stores. What matters is not who may or may not have been first, for there is no tidy chronology, but that the early stores were run by small family shopkeepers. It is often argued that they were a French concept. Certainly there is a place in any chronology for Aristide Boucicant, whose Bon Marché opened in

MARSHALL & SNELGROVE
334 to 348 OXFORD St
LONDON W.

COSTUMES
MANTLES
FURS LACE
GLOVES
CARPETS

NEW COSTUME DEPARTMENT

MANTLE DEPARTMENT

T SULMAN

Nothing has contributed to improve the
West End and other parts of London so
much as the continued recurrence of New
Buildings in the principal thoroughfares.
The block now illustrated was commenced
in 1875 and completed in 1878. Since that
period large and extensive premises in
Henrietta-street on the north, and Vere-
street on the east side have been added.
It is also in contemplation to shortly
rebuild the important block situated in
Marylebone-lane on the west angle.
When complete the whole structure,
north, south, east, west, will form
one of the finest and most attractive
range of warerooms in the
metropolis.

Paris in 1852 on the principle that shoppers could roam extensive premises displaying the widest range of merchandise marked with fixed prices, and the stock was, by 1863, segregated into clear departments from footwear to furnishings. Yet the records of British department stores show an even earlier trend towards segregation under one roof, and well before 1860 when William Whiteley constructed his purpose-built multi-department shop in Bayswater.

Bon Marché in Paris, nonetheless, was a decisive influence in store building in the late nineteenth century, and the opening in New York of Macys and Wanamakers drew on French experience, introducing lifts and full electrical lighting. The idea of raising trading from street level to as many as four or five floors derived from the experience of many individual shopkeepers, each seeing the possibilities for widening the provision of goods through single premises. Britain was not copying French or American experience, for the foundations of department stores were laid by the turn of the eighteenth century. Stores such as Bainbridge in Newcastle, Kendal Milne in Manchester, Lewis in Liverpool, Browns of Chester, Andersons of Glasgow, and Debenham & Freebody in London can claim to be pioneers. There were many others, some forgotten and casualties of their days. A special place is inevitable for Selfridges, the creation of a mercurial American, Gordon Selfridge, who proclaimed his great store to be a community centre and engaged in advertising in popular newspapers. Britain was strewn with stores with individual personalities and claims to be pioneers in their towns and cities.

And so the spread of provincial shopkeeping was ensured. It was to prove a massive training ground for young people who were destined to make their names in later years beyond local communities. But no less pertinent was the importance of all this in creating popular shopkeeping, eschewing London's preoccupation with the concept of luxury service to the aristocratic and upper middle class rich.

This was the epoch when the rich invested, the middle classes sought to ensure their comfort, and the labouring classes sought to obtain basic needs yet aspired to lower middle class status. It was a time when partnerships flourished and the first retailing companies made their appearance. Young men chose to go into trade as an honourable occupation. Retailing was not an easy life, but diligent hard work could be rewarded with a security not found in most jobs. Strong legs and a courteous manner were essentials.

The grand manner of design for the emporia which were erected in towns and suburban centres was no guarantee of success. What really mattered was the service and welcome given to customers and the selection of stock appropriate to the main source of custom. Prices and stock had to be adapted to the spending power of an increasing lower middle class. The selling rested with young men subjected to rigid discipline and long hours. They were trained with an iron hand.

One store put up a notice to shop assistants in 1854, for example, which required assistants to man their store the year round from 6 a.m until 9 p.m. Assistants had to sweep and dust, trim lamps, clean chimneys and even make pens. Any employee, it warned, 'who is in the habit of smoking Spanish cigars, getting shaved at a barber's shop, going to dances, and other such places of amusement will surely give his employer reason to be suspicious of his integrity and all-round honesty'. Each employee was required to give a guinea a year to church, and to attend Sunday School. Further, men were given one evening a week for courting purposes and two if they went to prayer meetings regularly. As an after-thought, the employer suggested that spare time be devoted to good literature (not an isolated thought since many shopkeepers developed special libraries for their staff).

The practice of staff living in was widespread. One Marshall & Snelgrove worker recorded his experiences for 1886. A wage of £5 a year was his reward. The 'living-in' system, in fact, offered many advantages to a boy from the country or without a London home. It provided some initial security, friendship and pocket money. As many as eleven men would share a bedroom of a house at the corner of London's Vere Street and Oxford Street. The lucky obtained four-bed rooms at Marylebone Lane. Single men generally slept in, and were allowed out on Saturday nights if they signed a book kept in the counting house and gave a counterfoil to the doorkeeper of the hostels.

Marshall & Snelgrove's Oxford Street store boasted a magnificent bearded head shopwalker, known behind his back as Pop. In frock coat, wide bell-bottomed trousers and patent boots – the whole outfit was set off by a black moiré silk waistcoat (white in summer) and a flower in his buttonhole–he ruled the roost muttering about standards as he checked someone or found any evidence of unapproved changes. In his bedroom at Vere Street, Pop would sometimes entertain apprentices with an organ recital. Over cakes and lemonade they would form a choir around him. Boots were placed outside bedrooms at night and cleaned by porters for collection by staff in the early hours when they rose for the day's trading. Apprentices often came from fairly well-to-do families, sometimes the sons of customers. At one time Marshall & Snelgrove charged a premium of sixty guineas, which was refunded over the three-year training period.

Employers' attitudes can be divined from a news report in *The Observer* of 18 December 1836, which records the fact that the principal linen drapers in Tottenham Court Road signed an agreement to close their shops at 8 p.m., except Saturday when they would stay open until 11 p.m.:

This arrangement which, it is hoped, will not be confined to the tradesmen in Tottenham Court Road, will have the effect of giving a generally energetic and intelligent class of men an opportunity of procuring recreation and improvements after the fatigues of the day, which is scarcely denied anywhere to mechanics and labourers.

There were basic rules for selling. Not atypical was one provincial drapery store which produced an 11-point guide for its assistants:

1   Be alert.
2   Stop all conversation with other workers when customers are present.
3   Stop all care of stock when a customer is present.
4   Smile and greet a customer pleasantly.
5   Look the customer in the eye.
6   Be eager to serve.

7   Be interested in the use of the merchandise.
8   Never glance knowingly at other fellow-workers because of the customer's appearance or the merchandise requested.
9   Present your sales book for signing pleasantly.
10 Serve the late customers politely.
11 Say 'Thank you', whether the customer buys or not.

Order, thrift, and discipline were the aims of Victorian shopkeepers. They represented a code elaborated by Samuel Smiles, reflecting the mood of this era. For its part, Debenhams saw these as virtues to be encouraged amongst its staff. By 1899 the directors had established a private fire brigade (later there was the Debenham Special Constabulary). Shopkeeping reflected social trends, too. By the late nineteenth century, power was still passing steadily to the people and with it went a relentless rise in the purchasing power of the wage earners in factory and office.

The *Reform Bill* of 1884 brought one vote, one value. Lord Salisbury deplored the 'placing of a great Empire under the absolute control of the poorest classes'. Joseph Chamberlain, the radical businessman and uncrowned king of Birmingham, replied:

Lord Salisbury constitutes himself the spokesman of a class – of the class to which he himself belongs, who toil not neither do they spin; whose fortunes – as in his case – have originated by grants made in times gone by for the services which courtiers rendered kings, and have since grown and increased, while they have slept, by levying an increased share on all that other men have done by toil and labour to add to the general wealth and prosperity of the country.

Arthur Balfour, a democrat and modern conservative, saw the need to extend responsibility to the whole community in the interests of national continuity. Few businessmen disagreed, least of all retailers whose power and influence had grown in town and city under Victoria and for whom *continuity* was a fourth universal sentiment to be added to Samuel Smiles's code to carry into the next century.

Lo Chamberlain to H.M. Queen Alexandra

*By Virtue of the authority
to me given, I do hereby appoint
Mr John Swayne Pearce of Regent Street
London for and on behalf of Waterloo
House & Swan & Edgar Silk Mercer
& Linen Draper*

in ordinary to Her Majesty.

*To hold the said Place so long
as shall seem fit to The Mistress of the Robes
for the time being.*

*This Warrant is strictly
personal and will become void on the Death,
Retirement, or Bankruptcy of any person
hereby appointed.*

*Given under my Hand this
5th day of July 1888 in the
51st Year of Her Majesty's Reign.*

L. S. Buccleuch

Mistress of the Robes.

4 'The most comfortable shop in the world'

*What a welter we should be in if the
politicians were to hand over the management
of public affairs to their critics.*

F. S. Oliver, *Endless Adventure*

At 6.36 p.m. on the night of 22 January 1901, Queen Victoria died at Osborne, her beloved Isle of Wight home. Her death sent even those who could not really afford the expense hurrying into drapers and dress shops to order thousands upon thousands of yards of black mourning crape. Debenhams' wholesale department was cleared of all its stocks. So heavy was the demand that Samuel Courtauld & Company, which for some time had been vainly trying to revive a flagging public interest in the etiquette of mourning with a cheaper crape 'for the socially less elevated end of the market', was probably saved from a serious financial crisis. The surge of sales bridged the time it needed to bring in coloured fabrics.

Three years later, Courtaulds, desperate for a replacement for its vanishing crape profits, bought patents for a viscose process for making artificial silks, later to be known to drapers and the world as rayon.

All this might seem a tasteless way to record the death of a great Queen. Yet it is one measure of the national emotion and reaction to a sovereign who gave the British such pride in themselves and encouraged the creation of the world's greatest Empire.

Victoria's reign was filled with soldiers and men and women of action, like Wellington, Livingstone, and Florence Nightingale. Her years were studded with great events, from the Charge of the Light Brigade and the great purchase of Suez Canal shares to renewed Irish troubles and the Boer War. A procession of no less than ten Prime Ministers, who kissed hands on forming nineteen administrations, from Lord Melbourne to Gladstone (four times), included 'my Dizzy', Benjamin Disraeli (later the Earl of Beaconsfield). She witnessed the end of Whigs and Tories, and the age of Liberal power clashing with modern Conservatism which was rooted in Burke's ideas.

The epoch was not without its thinkers and eminent men of letters. It might seem crass to try to link thinkers and men of letters with shopkeeping. Yet it is a curious fact that one of the leading advocates of Empire and Imperial power was a young man, Frederick Oliver, who not only took

Royal Warrant permitting Swan & Edgar to style themselves 'by appointment to the late Queen Victoria'

59

Debenhams into the Edwardian age, but also established himself as one of the cleverest political philosophers and writers of the time.

Britain's trading systems were an integral part of her social and politic history. Indeed, politicians had become preoccupied with the economics of free trade and mass distribution, even though historians linger on the wars royal events, and acts of foreign statesmanship.

That Debenham & Freebody became associated with a master thinker ab to combine shopkeeping with literature, and even political intrigue at th highest levels, is an unshakeable fact. The association of writers with stor management is not quite so odd as it might now seem. Victorian privat enterprise needed its philosophers and intellectuals to state the ethics tha they saw in competitive trading.

Private enterprise was not without its severe critics. Amongst them wa Thomas Hughes, author of *Tom Brown's School Days* and a great Christian Socialist, who found time, while serving as MP for Lambeth, for holdin high office in the cooperative movement. John Stuart Mill advocated reta organization by the working classes. On the centre ground stood Charle Dickens, the most popular writer of the nineteenth century. He found tim not only to caricature shopkeeping in his novels but wrote his own trenchar sketch:

Six or eight years ago, the epidemic began to display itself among the line drapers and haberdashers. The primary symptoms were an inordinate love of plate glass, and a passion for gas-lights and gilding. The disease gradually progressed, an at last attained a fearful height. Quiet, dusty old shops in different parts of tow were pulled down; spacious premises with stuccoed fronts and gold letters wer erected instead. Floors were covered with Turkey carpets, roofs supported by mas sive pillars; doors knocked into windows; a dozen squares of glass into one; on shopman into a dozen; and there is no knowing what would have been done if it ha not been fortunately discovered, just in time, that the Commissioners of Bankruptc were as competent to decide such cases as the Commissioners of Lunacy and that little confinement and gentle examination did wonders. The disease abated. It die away. A year or two of comparative tranquillity ensued. Suddenly it burst out agai amongst the chemists; the symptoms were the same, with the addition of a stron desire to stick the royal arms over the shop door, and a great rage of mahogany varnish, and expensive floor-cloth. Then the hosiers were infected, and began to pu down their shop fronts with frantic recklessness. The mania died away again, an the public began to congratulate themselves upon its entire disappearance, when burst forth with ten-fold violence among the publicans and keepers of 'wine-vaults' From that moment it has spread among them with unprecedented rapidity, exhibit ing a concatenation of all the previous symptoms; onward it has rushed to every par of the town knocking down all the old public-houses, and depositing splendi mansions, stone balustrades, rosewood fittings, immense lamps and illuminate clocks at the corner of every street.

Sketches by Boz

Frederick Scott Oliver, destined to become managing director and late deputy chairman of Debenhams, would have roared with delight at Dick ens's scepticism. Nonetheless, he did in time order in the demolition squad to the Debenham & Freebody store. Born in 1864, Oliver was a man of the rarest quality and it is a credit to Ernest Debenham's judgement that he recruited this eminent controversialist and political thinker to help run a drapery business in danger of losing its sense of direction, torn as it was between retailing and wholesaling. Oliver delighted in being called a draper and he saw no reason why Debenhams should not expand as major retailers as well as enlarging the wholesale business.

There can be no doubt that Debenhams' eventual pre-eminence in departmental store trading owes much to Oliver's decisive influence on both Frank and his son Ernest Debenham. Perhaps Oliver's name is now lost except to scholars of political literature, yet during his life glowing tributes were paid to his gifts as a writer by many leading figures. John Buchan, a close friend, stated: 'The ordinary citizen has never had a more eloquent defender, or the common politician, who as a rule is not overburdened with praise.'

If any single man understood the history of the times through which Debenhams had already passed, it was Oliver. Indeed, *The Times* on 26 November 1913 recorded that Oliver was 'one of the few men out of Parliament who have exercised in recent years a far greater influence on public thinking than the ordinary front bencher'.

The Cambridge-educated Oliver was a handsome, worldly person. His flashing mind and logic fascinated the more conservative Debenham. They had met at university, after which Oliver was called to the Bar in 1889. Nonetheless, he needed little temptation from Ernest Debenham to become a draper. They became firm friends as well as business partners, and, after incorporation, there came for Oliver a directorship and a good income to support his writing. Here then was an extraordinary man, able to combine a flair for retailing with literature and public affairs. The Debenhams revelled in Oliver's robust manner and his free speaking on any topic, marvelling at his rapid grasp of business practice and his constant challenges to established ways of trading.

The association between Oliver and Debenhams brought him a huge fortune, while the Debenhams basked in his fame and the closeness of such a man to the circles of power. It was exciting to know something about the eminent people they met as mere customers. Oliver was a constant source of gossip and his contacts with people in politics, law, and other walks of life helped keep the business alert to what was taking place in the important sectors of national life.

Initially, Oliver's legal training was of great help. Businessmen were, by now, in need of lawyers. Partnership had been the basis of controlling businesses such as Debenhams, but Victorian growth and development required reforms which radically altered the concept of family partnership and led on to corporate status for many enterprises.

Company development had been stopped after the passing of the *Bubble Act* in 1719. It became an indictable offence for companies to invite public subscriptions, to make stock transferable, or to act as a corporation other than by Royal charter. This Act remained in force until after the end of the Napoleonic Wars, when much capital became free for investment and a new situation therefore arose. In 1825, Parliament repealed the *Bubble Act,* and the unincorporated enterprises of Britain were treated as partnerships.

Debenhams was a partnership. As such, it could not sue or be sued unless all partners were joined in the legal action. Companies which grew with full or associate partners were greatly restricted in going to court, causing difficulties with debtors and suppliers. An Act passed in 1834 empowered the Crown to give unincorporated companies the right to take legal action in the name of nominated people. Both this Act and the law of 1825 were repealed in 1837 in favour of the important *Joint Stock Companies Act* 1844. Eleven years later saw enactment of the *Limited Liability Bill,* which set the important principle that joint stock companies could limit their liability to the amounts unpaid on their shares.

Another landmark was the *Companies Act* of 1862. This forbade any company or partnership to carry on business for gain unless it was registered.

Under these provisions Debenham & Freebody and Debenham & Company were registered as Debenham Limited in 1905 with a capital of £750 000 (£650 000 being 6 per cent Preferred and £100 000 carrying profits). No capital was offered to the public, but a profit-sharing arrangement involved reserving 20 per cent of the capital and nearly a third of profits for seven managing partners and staff. The seven were Edward Pipe, James Yeo, Edwin Ingram, C. H. Wren, George Milligan, J. Kitching, and Frederick H. Richmond.

The *Drapers' Record* on 4 February 1905 commented:

A feature of the change is that no professional promoter whatever has been connected with the conversion, a noteworthy point, as, needless to say, many an ambitious body of promoters had 'had its eye' on this successful business.

The name of Debenham is undoubtedly one of the household words of the soft goods trade, and it is to be hoped that its success of the past will be perpetuated in the future.

Oliver's arrival was quickly followed first by moves to establish a bigger presence in the top end of London's retail trade, and then a second phase of wheeling and dealing which was to create a great national chain of department stores, embracing the well established county set customers and including popular traders competing with attractive fixed prices for an ever widening range of stock.

The rise of newer and more fashionable West End stores such as Marshall & Snelgrove had attracted away some important customers. A need to restore Debenham & Freebody's snob appeal had led to the decision in 1896 to buy Nicholays, the oldest fur business in London, holding Royal Warrants from Queen Victoria and reigning families in Russia, Austria, Prussia, Belgium and Spain.

The custom of people with social and court-related pretensions was secured by winning the patronage of the new King Edward VII and Queen Alexandra as well as the then Prince of Wales (later George V) and the Princess of Wales (later Queen Mary). Stunning presentation gowns, evening wear, garden party dresses, travelling costumes and tea gowns were turned out by special designers from new workrooms and fitted by French and English trained experts. Bespoke tailors looked after the menswear.

Messrs. Wm & Chas Brown & Co

You are hereby appointed

Silk Mercer

to Her Royal Highness The Princess of Wales.

Given under my hand and seal
at Marlborough House,
this 8th day of Nov. 1869

Aaron's

Chamberlain

Messrs. W. and C. Brown and Co

You are hereby appointed

Silk Mercers in Chester

to His Royal Highness The Prince of Wales.

Given under my hand and seal
at Marlborough House,
this First day of November 1869

Comptroller

Messrs W. & C. Brown & Co
...tend to any further

Above left and right: *Royal warrants
granted to Browns of Chester in 1869*

Right: *Letter from the Queen's
lady-in-waiting ordering lace from
Griffin & Spalding, 1911*

WINDSOR CASTLE

February 1st 1911.

The Lady in Waiting
is commanded by
the Queen to inform
Messrs Griffin & Spalding
that she is much
pleased with the
specimens of lace
they sent her and
has made the
~~following~~ enclosed selection.

Artist's impression of the rebuilt Debenham & Freebody store

But one outstanding problem remained – the existing buildings of Debenham & Freebody were entirely inadequate for the image and were below the standards of other rival premises. Records for the time use the descriptions 'rambling and inconvenient' and 'entirely inadequate'. After intensive argument about the finance required, it was agreed to demolish the existing buildings and 'to rebuild them from the foundations on a very different scale'. Architects William Wallace and James Gibson were called in to design a grand store with the very latest in customer comforts, from new Otis lifts to an elegant restaurant and gentlemen's smoking rooms. There was a ladies' club room adjoining a suite of dressing and retiring rooms with magazines, telephones and postal services. George Trollope & Sons constructed the building, starting in February 1906 and undertaking it in sections.

Rebuilding brought an air of excitement to the staff as it caught the mood of a return to retailing on a grand scale. To pay for the work were the rising profits of the wholesale business. Debenhams Ltd was now formed to own Debenham & Freebody at arm's length along with Debenham & Co (wholesalers, manufacturers, and shippers). Principal property leases were held direct from the Howard de Walden estates for 999 years, an 'unexampled fixity' of tenure with nominal ground rents.

New men were now brought in to join the master board – Samuel Figgis, James Yeo, and, notably. Mr (later Sir) Frederick H. Richmond. Profits of

64

the main parent company were relatively small, at around £40 000–£50 000 a year until the rebuilt store could make its impact. The financial effect of the new store was such that a great gamble had been taken with the whole enterprise.

The new store had to exude luxury and comfort so that the highest prices could be obtained from a clientèle preoccupied with buying the best.

Luxury is surely a frame of mind. Those provincial Victorian shopkeepers who admired the skills of West End houses and built replicas of London departmental stores did not necessarily understand why such premises appeared a prerequisite for selling goods which might be regarded as luxury articles. They extolled to their employees the prevailing virtues of thrift and hard work yet never for one moment thought that the daily parade before the staff of people in pursuit of luxury might breed envy and resentment. That there never appeared any antagonism at the points of sale was probably due to the feeling of continuity and security which everyone felt within the surroundings of a well appointed store.

Nice things sold in surroundings of the greatest comfort could arouse the fantasies of the sales person, just as much as those of the customer with the ability to buy. To enter Debenham & Freebody's store, for example, was to pass into another world where luxury could be smelt, felt, and seen. The approach of the sales people exuding the impression that their means and knowledge were equal to madam's was the signal for a ritual role playing. True feelings were often suppressed between customer and servant, though each demonstrated many emotions amid the play of manners.

An American economist of the time, Thorstein Veblen, observed that the leisured classes indulged in what he described as 'conspicuous consumption'. The department stores, patronized by the rich and their leisured wives, offered customers satisfaction both by the purchase of goods which might make an impression on others and by confirming their status before a helpful assistant unable to criticize directly their eventual choice and always open to the customer's censure, whether deserved or not. Profit from luxury was dependent on suborning the customer into a certain frame of mind, essentially concerned with self-satisfaction.

Fine stores made it acceptable for social conscience and Victorian virtues to be temporarily suppressed by the sheer delight to be derived from touching and examining the best merchandise in well appointed surroundings. Many purchases were a triumph of individual indulgence and impulse. The customer's satisfaction was different from that of the craftsmen, artists, and manufacturers involved in the supply of articles which offered high quality and what was known as good taste. Discreet assistants cultivated in the customer a feeling that their skill was one of discernment.

High fashion goods or expensive furnishings were, in fact, pre-selected by buyers, and salesmanship might make an item described as a luxury a necessity, a contradiction of terms but surely the reason why luxury cannot be defined as mindless extravagance. Price was important to the shopkeeper for the profit to be earned, yet it could be of secondary importance for a customer examining some fine model gown.

In choosing an article the decision could not be based on a high price as a

Coat and skirt salon

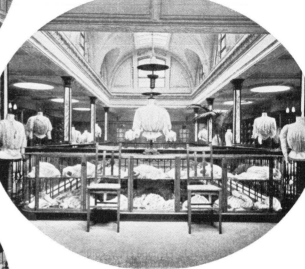

Blouse salon

Untrimmed millinery and flowers

Lingerie salon

guarantee of satisfaction. The price had to be an expression of quality or exclusivity but was not necessarily a guide to good judgement. This was not always fully understood by the nouveau riche, otherwise simple dresses might just as well be labelled 'This Dress Has Cost Sixty Guineas'. What mattered was that the dress looked as if it cost sixty guineas, yet was a statement of individual discernment rather than income. A customer, to adapt an Americanism, had to feel like sixty guineas, not look like sixty guineas.

Placing the customer in the appropriate frame of mind required skills in buying, salesmanship, and store design. The Debenham & Freebody store in Wigmore Street was a manifestation of the unconscious and conscious desires of all who entered its marble entrance hall. Its atmosphere was pervasive and influenced its manager, Frederick Richmond, for the rest of his career in the setting of standards for departmental storekeeping.

Faced externally in Doulton's Carrara ware, the new store was entered through a spacious entrance hall lined with cool grey-green and white marbles. On either side were huge showrooms and facing the entrance, manned by liveried doormen, was the marble staircase to upper floors. Oak woodwork, modelled ceilings, and soft green and grey carpets had been chosen for 'an unobtrusive but rich effect'. Bronze metal work was everywhere, on lamps and balustrading. Otis installed the very latest in gate lifts, Ozonair put in an air purification system, and a vacuum steam system provided a 'complete change of washed and warmed air three times per hour'.

The pride of Richmond was evident in a contemporary brochure in which he invited visitors to the Franco-British Exhibition to visit what he called 'the most comfortable shop in the world'.

Everywhere you will find the evidence of two fundamental principles – the comfort and convenience of our customers, and the taste and value of our goods.

You will feel at home on entering the doors and appreciate the quiet, restful atmosphere – everything orderly and conveniently displayed to advantage in the spacious, light, airy rooms, decorated so as to form an appropriate setting for the goods themselves.

You may visit the various departments, then, if you wish, have lunch or tea at very moderate charges in the quiet, elegant Restaurant, to which a Smoking-room and Gentlemen's Cloak Room are attached.

The Ladies' Club Room, which adjoins a luxuriously appointed suite of Dressing and Retiring Rooms, is open to lady visitors, who may there read the papers and magazines, telephone, write letters, or meet their friends. Parcels and letters may be addressed to the Cloak Room.

As practical furriers, we buy all our own skins, which are made up, by a staff of skilled workers, into an extensive stock, ranging from muffs and stoles at moderate prices, to the richest sable garments costing 5000 guineas. The introduction of a system of freezing storage for preserving and prolonging the life of furs has proved of great benefit and convenience to customers.

As Court dressmakers, the house of Debenham & Freebody has long been noted for the creation of the most beautiful presentation gowns, wedding gowns, evening gowns, garden party dresses, visiting costumes and tea gowns, which are modelled by exclusive designers, are made in our own workrooms, and fitted by French and English fitters.

The distinctive features of our tailor-made costumes are the smart cut and the perfect tailoring given by the men tailors.

The large and varied selection of the newest Paris models on view in our Millinery Salon, upon the first floor, enables any customer to find a smart and becoming hat of exclusive design, and there is also upon the ground floor a popular-priced department for ready-trimmed hats, as well as an extensive department for untrimmed hats, flowers, feathers and ornaments of every description.

The high favour with which Lingerie Gowns have been received has led us to introduce a stock of the most exclusive models. These light and dainty gowns can be had from moderate to very high prices, according to the material and the amount of handwork.

Feather Neckwear is one of our specialities, and in this department we have an unusual range of boas in real ostrich, coque and marabout feathers, as well as capes and novelties. We stock boas to match costumes in all the fashionable shades and also in two-colour combinations.

The Corset department is under the control of a highly-skilled corsetière of exceptional experience and ability, so that ladies, even when purchasing quite inexpensive ready-to-wear corsets, know that their wants are being supplied by an expert, who will see that they get just what is suitable to their figures. The manageress makes a special study of the individual requirements of each customer, and sees that they are fitted with corsets that are really suitable as regards comfort, fit and style. She sees every customer herself, and in the case of special orders fits them herself.

The success of our Lingerie is due to the taste and refinement which characterizes every article, whether simple or elaborate. All the newest styles and most charming designs are to be seen.

In addition to our large stock of modern Laces, we hold also a unique collection of choice and costly antique Spanish, Italian, and Brussels lace. Many of these rare examples appeal to the connoisseur and the collector.

We always hold a large and well chosen stock of all kinds of silken, woollen and cotton fabrics, sold by the yard, and our system of sending out pattern-books to customers greatly adds to their convenience in shopping.

Our Gloves are made from specially selected skins, and carefully cut so as to avoid splitting and to stand the strain of usage.

The Ladies' and Children's Boot and Shoe department includes footwear for every possible occasion, in the smartest shapes and best materials.

The finest Irish, Scotch and French Linens in original designs are shown in one of our largest and best stocked departments.

We undertake special embroidery, all of it executed in England, including designs for Court trains and richly-trimmed gowns. At all times many examples of the exquisite handiwork of the Royal School are on exhibition upon our premises.

Our collection of Antiques is difficult to describe, as each piece has a distinctive character of its own. Of all the objects of antique interest in which we deal, old embroideries and brocades have for many years been the most important; but in addition a number of fine specimens, Sheffield plate, antique jewellery, cut glass furniture, china, pewter, and brasses of different periods will appeal to lovers of rare and choice things.

In November, 1900, we added to our own the stock and organization of the famous department of this character so long carried on by Howell & James in South Regent Street.

While the Country Order department is not seen, its efficiency is keenly felt by the customer, who benefits by its prompt and careful attention. Illustrated catalogues issued for the various departments are sent free on application, and most of our goods are sent on approval.

Shoppers in Regent Street, 1906 Radio Times Hulton Picture Library

Edwardian fashions Black satin evening wrap

In the selection of all our goods we have struck a note which is maintained throughout the establishment. Nothing is offered for sale that is not of good quality and refined in taste. Equal attention is given to the buying of every article, whether it be a reel of silk or the costliest fur coat.

No visitor can depart without having felt the advantages of the personnel of our staff. With the greatest care and attention we have gathered them about us as we grew, and we feel that they maintain a high standard of courtesy and attention.

In 1907, an exclusive Debenham & Freebody evening gown was priced at 16½ guineas. A rich opera coat cost £4. 18s. 6d. and a Japanese Kimono 5s. 6d. (4½ guineas in silk).

Much has been written about the emancipation of women, yet few writers have considered the struggle against the serge skirt, velvet blouse, flannel under-garments, metal and whalebone corsets and laced boots. The development of lighter clothes and freer expression was, nonetheless, concerned with freedom to become of significance in an economy where women sought a higher status, careers, and an end to confinement in uniforms and costumes by a male dominated society.

The influence of department stores on fashion in clothing was profound. While it was a necessity of life, like food and shelter, clothing had long been home made, sometimes purchased second-hand, or perhaps ordered from a local dressmaker or tailor. Early department stores implanted among their customers the creed that clothes might be replaced because they were out-of-date, rather than worn out. They moulded the desires of a middle class with sufficient money to improve wardrobes by the purchase of fashionable clothes. Fashion did not have to be the sole preserve of a rich élite.

From the mid-nineteenth century department stores catered for a rising demand for both ready-made and bespoke clothes. They employed teams of buyers who understood design, colour, style, accessories, and knew how to

69

Edwardian fashions

Leghorn hat

Serge cycling costume

Braided coat and skirt with blouse trimmed with écru lace and sequin

display garments, whether in printed catalogues, or on the sales floors. Customers trusted the buyers' expertise. The first fashion buyers placed orders with clothing manufacturers and, as in the case of Debenham & Freebody, a store might provide its own workrooms to cut, stitch, and sew fabrics into ever widening ranges of garments and accessories. In its hey-day, Debenham & Freebody were principally manufacturers and wholesalers with showrooms. In the main retail store there were 600 members of staff, but a further 3000 operated in workrooms and order departments, handling everything from the despatch of hats to ladies in rural homes to the submission to Queen Victoria of designs for Court presentation dresses.

Fashionable clothing cascaded from Victorian shopkeepers. The élite might still order their custom-made clothes and demand the latest Paris modes, but the Victorians in general, from cradle to grave, were kept supplied with a flood of capes, bootakins, gaiters, mantles, clouds, tippets, mitts, frillets, infantees and dresses. Hosiery and underwear became items of high fashion, and went on open display. Department stores steamed felt into millinery and pinned hats with novelties and feathers, creations which were frequently an unashamed self-indulgence. Children were among the first to wear ready-made elasticated fitted costumes, factory-made in large quantities.

Large-scale production of ready-to-wear clothing represented a considerable investment of capital and skills, whether undertaken in workrooms or factories. It was necessary to the continuity of bulk output that clothing should be bought regularly by large segments of the population. Discarded clothes maintained employment and profitability. The durability of women's clothes did not always rank high in the minds of Victorian ladies. Customers began to look for more style and character in their clothing as incomes improved. Newer fabrics and various decorative materials previously offered as 'novelties' allowed much scope to designers attempting to prove their ideas.

A machine room at Debenhams' Nottingham factory

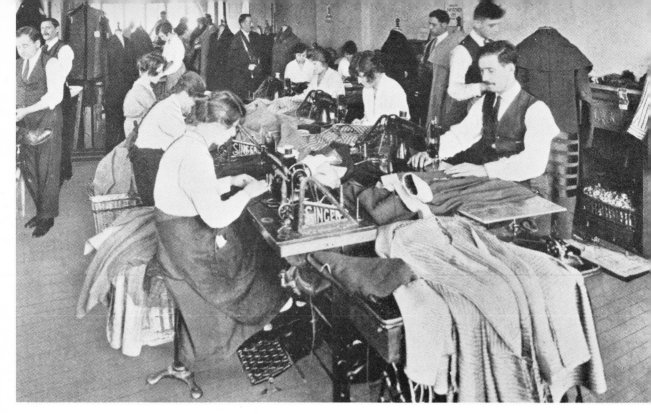

Debenhams' tailor-made work-room

The many workrooms within department stores gradually engaged in the preparation of stock during slack times for what became seasonable trends in clothing sales. This covered the decline in bespoke orders. Department stores made the once vulgar practice of 'price ticketing' respectable and this assisted the idea of ready-made clothes. Buyers engaged in personal predictions of future fashion requirements, and their stores started to stage shows, using their own mannequins, to display the latest lines. This fostered the view that stores were up-to-date with their styles and ideas, perhaps with less expensive versions of the clothes presented by great Paris and London designers.

Innovation in clothing, of course, moved as fast as the producers and converters of yarns came up with new ideas. All yarns, whether natural or, later, made by man, comprise fibres or filaments with distinctive properties for their spinning and weaving into cloth. The basic materials of *haute couture* in London or Paris at the turn of the century had been more or less the same as those found in the courts of the Pharaohs. All the now familiar artificial fibres came within living memory.

A typical product developed under a trade name was Hollins' 'Viyella', originally promoted for its texture and weight among better class retailers at what were very high prices. Such fabrics, when they appeared, were usually first available only to the rich. Garments made with a new cloth could attract a premium, and suppliers like Hollins even took action against department stores which attempted to reduce the price they sought to maintain as a mark of exclusivity and quality.

Trade catalogues bristling with sketches of clothes were eagerly studied by customers. The arrival of aniline dyestuffs in the mid-nineteenth century brought a greater variety of colours to textiles and made a dramatic impact on both the technology and design of cloth. In 1837, Marshall & Snelgrove

Reception dress with gun-metal embroidery
Debenhams, autumn 1909

Above: *Japanese jacket Debenhams' 1908 Souvenir Catalogue*

Opposite left: *Model evening gown Debenhams' 1908 Souvenir Catalogue*
Opposite right: *Restaurant or opera coat Debenhams' 1908 Souvenir Catalogue*

Evening gown
Debenhams, autumn 1909

The Hornet

Incroyable

The Witch

Debenhams, fancy dress design 1887

Paris Model Afternoon dresses Debenhams' autumn 1914

The new styles in fur capes and coats Debenhams' autumn 1914

Advertisement for Swan & Edgar, early 1900s

had departments specializing in traditional shawls, ball dresses, and muslin robes, but fifty years later the stock was transformed into a blaze of colour and greater variety. Magazines, such as *Lady's World*, turned to such stores in search of the latest designs and garments. To be up-to-date was to be smart. Marshall & Snelgrove bathing costumes in brightly striped flannelette with separate trousers and bodices, for example, were daring innovations at a time when early sea bathers preferred thick serge.

The advent of colour in printing and advances in engraving enabled stores to produce mail order catalogues which today are considered works of art. A sweeping Debenham & Freebody morning costume in all its full length glory, sewn from brown satin-de-laine with a wool fringed bustle and set off by a fancy bonnet was breathtaking to behold on dummy or in print. Trends could sweep the country through department stores. By 1912, the 'Empire' shape was adopted, for example, and department stores poured out Empire evening gowns and dresses, with chemises in gauze trimmed with torchon lace. Materials grew bolder. Brocades using surface rayon weft over a cotton warp became very popular, followed by suede-de-chine rayon and cotton crapes. Underwear, stockings, and frilled nightwear became lighter, and women started to give as much attention to such purchases as to frocks and outerwear. Lingerie and dresses utilized rayon jappes, and satins and maro-cains. Corsetry was greatly improved as elastics arrived. Early rayon was very expensive, and garments using the material reflected the high price as late as 1928. Viscose and cellulose acetate rayons were originally mixed with cotton, and later cellulose acetate fibres allowed cross-dyed shot effects which enhanced their use for fashion goods.

Department stores could not cope on their own and new fashion chain stores sought supplies of clothes, too. Many small firms began to specialize in making batches of garments, using new or improved machinery requiring skilled operatives. Their products were readily taken up by shopkeepers, either by direct ordering or through travelling wholesalers. Department stores developed a breed of buyers able to assess samples and to back their judgements with appropriate orders. Ready-made clothing might be ordered to carry the store's name, or that of the supplier hoping to develop a reputation for good design, colour, and anticipation of style. London's East End and parts of Leeds, Manchester, Nottingham, and Leicester had their concentrations of producers of fashion clothing, known as the 'Rag Trades', full of people able to turn out speculative designs or make up orders to specifications laid down by buyers.

Clearly Debenhams' magnificent store was a symbol of the status and traditions of the family in London's central trading districts, of which Mayfair was pre-eminent. Telephone services were developing fast, not only for personal communications but for dealing with customers. When the Post Office decided to open in 1902 one of the first major manual exchanges outside the City of London, it selected Bird Street, off Oxford Street, for its Mayfair operations. Among the first business subscribers in 1903, was Debenhams which was rewarded with an historic telephone number, Mayfair One. No customer, or anyone with business dealings, could ever forget such a number, and it was the envy of rivals.

73

Shoppers at Swan & Edgar, 1912 Radio Times Hulton Picture Library

By now it was becoming clear that the various enterprises in retailing had begun to enter the realms of big business. History tells us that many people were, at this time, founding great businesses – by the start of the Great War there were 100 Marks & Spencer stores, multiple tailors, such as Hepworths and a new chemists' trade pioneered by Boots and Timothy Whites. Some sixteen concerns, including Singer Sewing, and W. H. Smith, boasted more than 200 branches each by 1914. When Debenhams Ltd was formed in 1905 there were over 15 000 multiple shops, mainly footwear and food (Maypole Liptons and Home & Colonial Tea, being some examples of contemporary names). At the death of Queen Victoria, the Cooperative movement alone had 1464 local societies and its trade doubled from £50 000 000 a year to £100 000 000 in fourteen years and doubled yet again to £200m in the succeeding five years. As for department stores, statistics are scant, but there were 250 by 1914 handling 2½ per cent of national retail trade.

Mass shopkeeping was on its way and prestigious department stores had to find their role. It was all very well Debenhams helping to supply robes for King Edward's coronation or the opening of his first Parliament, but the profits of the future rested with serving all sections of society. At first Debenhams saw its future best secured by the continuing development of wholesaling to others, while specializing in the fashionable London trade it knew best.

The time came when it capitalized on its name and took luxury to the masses. The world was changing fast. New aviators were in the news – Bleriot crossed the channel in 1909, six years after the Wright brothers' epic flight in America signalled that nation's challenge to British industrial and inventive power. No less significant than Bleriot's exploit was the introduction of old age pensions.

74

Shoppers at Swan & Edgar, 1912

This was an age of capital and new City merchant banking skills. It spawned a breed of financiers interested in creating and expanding companies serving mass markets. In 1908, Debenhams thought itself big when it raised its capital to £1 million, though net profits slumped to £38 816 15s. 10d. because the wholesale side was experiencing a decline in sales rates that augured badly for manufacturers. The new store brought a recovery and by 1910 net profits exceeded £100 000 on the £1m issued capital.

At this point the death of King Edward ushered in the reign of George V, and within two years, in 1912, the ageing Frank Debenham retired at 77, leaving Ernest Debenham and his friend Oliver, as well as Richmond, a completely free hand. Europe, disunited and dominated by ruling families, was in a strange mood, her power was under direct challenge from a New World. With half a dozen great cultures, it had in the previous century sent 40 000 000 people overseas. For her part Britain invested £4 billion in other parts of the world, while France had become a great world banker.

Europe now made 60 per cent of world steel and three in every four merchant ships flew her flags. Half the coal came from her mines, mostly British. Yet there was a symbolic disaster in the year of Frank Debenham's resignation – the pride of British engineering and luxury, the *Titanic* sank on her way to North America with the loss of 1517 lives. In that year, the United States made 485 000 motor vehicles compared with 25 000 in Britain. Europe was more interested in armies than cars for the masses. Nearly 4m men were kept under arms. They still rode horses and drew swords, even though the machine gun had long been invented. While Einstein was working on his theory of relativity, there was a lust for lost power and violent change. Kaiser Wilhelm and Lenin were but two extremes of demagogic statements and intrigue.

75

It was as if a new order in Europe had to come from war. Meanwhile the New World embraced mass production with the oppressed and driftwood of the world's population, including millions of European immigrants. The French would finance Russia's war with Japan while military expenditure drained Germany. Then on a summer's day, 28 June 1914, as shoppers thronged Oxford Street, came news of an assassination – of the Archduke Franz Ferdinand of Habsburg-Este, heir to the Austro-Hungarian throne. In little over a month, on 5 August 1914, the pride of London's society began pouring into recruiting offices set up in Great Scotland Yard. The night before an American novelist, in a letter to a friend, wrote: 'The taper went out last night.'

The horror of the Great War is no subject for this book. But Debenhams had an unusual place, for its managing director was the acknowledged advocate for military conscription, and visited generals at the Front. The company lost its horses and vehicles – and its finest men on alien roads, in trenches, and amid the mud of no-man's-land. Hundreds of employees died by bullet, shell and gas in those terrible years, and today the role of honour is still displayed in glass-encased books recording the brave men, and women, who went out in a steady flow between 1914 and 1918 to die for Europe's blind folly.

In the summer of 1914 young men came from weekend houses, from the Notts versus Surrey cricket match at the Oval, and from suburban terraced houses to sign away their lives. They went to war whistling the tunes of the current show at the Alhambra, knowing how to dance the new tango. In boaters sold by Debenham & Freebody, thousands of young men thronged the Mall singing, carried away by the excitement of a prospective war that started with cavalry and horse-drawn omnibuses and finished with tanks, aerial bombs, and submarines.

Swan & Edgar on the outbreak of war

The Great War, which brought excess profits duty, was to drive two great London stores into each other's arms as it made its economic impact. By 1916 it was evident things were becoming difficult. Londoners had been attempting to continue the old life, to the anger of the returning injured, and the families of the millions who died. Luxury stores later found custom dwindling and marked changes in social habits. Officer classes were thrown with private soldiers into the closer relationships which were inevitable with common danger and the hypocrisy of the military leaders of a country ill-equipped for total warfare. The eventual arrival of less inhibited Americans in Europe's bloody conflict further exposed the worst excesses of the English class system.

In March 1916, Textile Securities was formed and a 'working relationship' established with Marshall & Snelgrove, now in financial trouble for the first time in its seventy-nine years of unbroken trading. Textile Securities was set up, with Treasury approval, to buy a big block of shares held by three Debenham directors and all the shares of Marshall & Snelgrove. The idea was to work jointly to preserve the retail operations in wartime, when Debenhams was proving a more successful operation. That year, profits after provisions were £237 797 for Debenhams and only £57 170 for Marshall & Snelgrove. Within one year, mutual stock-buying and reforms of Marshall & Snelgrove policies doubled the latter's profits, while those of Debenhams remained the same. It was clear that the war was disrupting overseas trade and operations across the world.

Troops in the field received small gifts from the board and some news. Christmas 1917 brought letters hand-signed by Ernest Debenham, who was later knighted. The following letter was received by Private McCabe, serving in France. It was accompanied by a long list of staff who had given their lives and, across the years, it may seem to lack sensitivity.

Debenham & Company,
(*DEBENHAMS LIMITED*)

Telegrams, 'Debenham, Wire London'   *91, Wimpole Street*
Telephone No. 1 Mayfair, (40 lines)   *London, W.*

                             December, 1917
Pte. C. H. McCabe, 391919.
  France.

Dear McCabe,
    I am writing once again to send you the good wishes both of my colleagues upon the Board of Debenhams Limited and myself.
    The past year has seen no event of marked interest in connection with the business. Trade, however, is still satisfactory, although increasingly difficult by reason of the growing scarcity of supplies and the steady drain upon our more experienced male staff for military service.
    You will be interested to learn that no fewer than 1071 of the male staff of the Company and Marshall & Snelgrove Ltd. to date have joined the Forces,

leaving only 12 A and B.1 men. These few have been exempted by the Authorities by reason of their absolute indispensability to the maintenance of the two businesses.

I am sorry to say that during the year 23 of your old colleagues have died in the service of their Country making in all 89 since the outbreak of war. I am enclosing a list of these, also of those who have been decorated for conspicuous service and of others promoted to commissioned rank.

It is with deep regret I also have to advise you that Mr John Marshall, one of your Directors, who obtained a Commission in the 2/9th County of London Regiment (Queen Victoria Rifles) has been missing since September 26th, when he took part in an attack. To date no news has been obtained of him and we can only trust he has been made a prisoner and that he may safely return to us at the termination of the war.

In considering our plans for the re-instatement of such of you as were employed by the Company prior to the outbreak of war, and to whom as you know we gave an undertaking to take back should you desire to return to us, we are all impressed with the importance of ensuring that no man should resume his duties until perfectly fit to do so. To this end we propose that every man upon his return shall be examined by our doctor, and in such cases as the doctor may advise a rest, it shall be the endeavour of the Company to give such assistance as will render it possible for the necessary holiday or treatment to be taken.

I would like to make it clear that this proposal is made in your own interest. For example, a man suffering from heart or nervous strain, by an over anxiety which led him to resume prematurely his civilian career might easily jeopardise his health for life. Again, should anyone be suffering from tuberculosis, if taken in time probably a cure could be effected; whereas if neglected the disease would be a source of danger both to himself and his colleagues. I would add that the examination will be a private matter between the doctor and the man himself, and that the Company will only be concerned in the best means of restoring to health anyone found to be unfit.

In conclusion I would remind you that I shall always be pleased to hear from you, and that we are all anxious to keep in as close a touch as is possible with our men away on service.

We are posting under separate cover a small parcel which I trust will be safely received in time for Christmas.

With best wishes for the coming year and your safe return.

Yours faithfully,

ERNEST R. DEBENHAM

[Author's note: Underlining was in original letter]

There can be no doubt that Debenham was well informed about the war, for his unusual managing director, Frederick Oliver, made a visit to the Front in 1917, when the British offensive and the Passchendael operations were just starting. Indeed, he was invited to help revise Sir Roger Keyes's famous Zeebrugge despatch. Letters now available show Oliver predicting submarine warfare when the war was just a few months old, seeing the importance of the French General Foch, urging a separate organization for military supplies, and predicting a War Cabinet six months before it was set up. On the Tsar's abdication he quoted Dilke's remark that the only revolution possible in Russia would be one which transferred autocratic power from one emperor to another.

Oliver, who knew General Haig, was an intriguer and pamphleteer. He was a member of the Monday Night Cabal which unseated Asquith and paved the way for Lloyd George's leadership of the war. His homes in Berkshire and Scotland were the scene of many weekend parties attended by powerful figures in Whitehall. One friend was Professor G. M. Trevelyan, the great historian, who spoke of Oliver's 'matchless conversation' with an intellectual power 'tempered with a quaint sweet humour, testifying to the breadth and kindliness that underlay his revolt against sentiment'. Oliver was to depict the events and course of the war in regular letters to his brother in British Columbia.

Another instance of how Ernest Debenham might, on looking back, have seemed insensitive comes to light in one record of a company meeting after the Armistice. He declared: 'The firm's experience is that those men who had served in the forces were more efficient because of that experience.' And yet this was clearly seen at the time as a tribute to ex-soldiers returning to retailing to compete with those who had stayed behind.

Military records show scores of London store staff who won medals for gallantry. Debenhams' stores had a notable record, quite above average for similar sized business houses. The loss of life was commemorated with a staff remembrance ceremony and notice to staff. Records of the fallen have been kept with meticulous care.

One death during 1917 was that at 80 of Frank Debenham, who had finally left the board three years before, several years after handing the chairmanship to his son, Ernest. War had led to disorganization of the great foreign trade developed by Frank Debenham, who liked to be known as 'an old laceman' rather than a master shopkeeper. Lace buying was always a first love and he monitored others with a closeness not far short of devotion.

Whatever the disruption of Continental exports and losses of foreign currency, Debenhams concentrated on retailing and war did not hold up innovation. A gifts trade was started, and a new idea was a department specializing in perfumes and toiletries, normally the sideline of chemists and druggists. Fragrances, toilet waters, and perfumes were ideal lines and manufactured cosmetics were a natural extension later. Wholesale perfumiers were eager to obtain the business of the great stores, which in turn earned 33⅓ per cent profit on their products.

Perfumery departments became crowded with women, and sales staff were persuasive, using sample-and-nose techniques. It was sensible for the products to be sold by the stores where they bought dresses and personal clothing of all kinds. There was a sense of service which the busy chemists did not always offer. Women had begun to enter the retail trade in great numbers during the Great War and, like the men, underwent severe apprenticeships. A typical example of an indenture signed about this time with a provincial storekeeping enterprise, not then in Debenhams' ownership, was as follows:

79

Indentures of apprenticeship, 1917

This Indenture Witnesseth That Cicely Winifred Colyer of 9, The Parade, Folk tone in the County of Kent with the consent and approbation of her sister He Roberts (married woman) of 29 Somerset Road, Ashford in the County of K (testified by her being a party to and executing these presents) doth put hers Apprentice to PLUMMER RODDIS Limited of Folkestone.

Drapers, to learn their Art, and with them, after the manner of an Apprentice, serve from the Thirteenth day of May, One Thousand Nine Hundred and Sevente unto the full end and term of Three years from thence next following to be fu complete and ended. During which term the said Apprentice her Masters faithfu shall serve, their secrets keep, their lawful commands everywhere gladly do, s shall do no damage to her said Masters, nor see to be done of others, but to I power shall tell or forthwith give warning to her said Masters of the same, she sh not waste the goods of her said Masters, nor lend them unlawfully to any, she sh not contract matrimony within the said term, nor play at cards or dice tables, or a other unlawful games, whereby her said Masters may have any loss with their o goods or others during the said term, without license of her said Masters sh neither buy nor sell, she shall not haunt taverns or playhouses, nor absent hers from her said Masters' service day or night unlawfully, but in all things, as a faith Apprentice, she shall behave herself towards her said Masters and all theirs duri the said term.

And the said Helen Roberts hereby covenants with the said PLUMMER ROD Limited, that all the covenants on the part of the Apprentice hereinbefore contair shall be duly performed and observed, and that she, the said Helen Roberts v provide the Apprentice with proper and sufficient wearing apparel during the s term. And the said PLUMMER RODDIS Limited hereby covenant with the said He Roberts and with the said Apprentice that they will train their said Apprentice in Art which they use, by the best means that they can, shall teach and instruct, cause to be taught and instructed, finding unto the said Apprentice sufficient me drink and lodging, during the said term, provided always, and it is hereby agree that if the Apprentice shall commit any breach of the covenant on her part hereinl fore contained, or shall in the opinion of the Masters be unsuitable or unfit for business, or conduct or progress be unsatisfactory, the Masters may immediat cancel this Indenture.

And for the true performance of all and every the said Covenant and Agreeme either of the said parties bindeth themselves unto the other by these presents, A Witness whereof the parties above named to these Indentures interchangeably h: put their hands and seals the Thirteenth day of May and in the Seventh Year of Reign of our Sovereign George V, by the Grace of God of the United Kingdom Great Britain and Ireland, and of the British Dominions beyond the Seas, K Defender of the Faith, and in the Year of our Lord One Thousand Nine Hundr and Seventeen.

Sixty-one years later, the signatory, now a Mrs Cotton, lives quietly in apartment at Hastings and can recall with great clarity the formal ceremo whereby she received on 13 May 1917 her indentures. She was then aged 1 and had to swear on oath, before the assembled directors of the Folkesto store, to serve loyally and diligently. As an apprentice, she was paid 1s. week, (the entry fee cost parents a £25 premium in 1917). At the end of l training, she was offered a post at a salary of £30 a year as a showroc assistant. But such was the quality of her apprenticeship over three years a the proof of the indentures, that she was able to leave and to take a post another store at £60 a year.

'The apprenticeship was hard, but something of which I was later very proud,' she explained. 'The thoroughness with which we were taught all manner of things, including how to sell and to give service with courtesy, really fitted apprentices with skills for life. Today, I still know every kind of material, all the types of cloth, fitting, how to fold clothes, preparation of stock, and matters ranging from buying to display duties.'

Plummer's store at Folkestone ran a hostel for its staff and, in her time, Mrs Cotton's housekeepers were two strict Baptist ladies who firmly bolted the doors every evening around 9.30 p.m. and, unfailingly, reported every infraction of the rigid rules of discipline.

There was no more graphic demonstration to Mrs Cotton of discipline than an example involving her own sister, also taken into apprenticeship, and who was seen on the then pierhead skating rink when off duty. She was warned that nice Plummer's girls did not allow themselves to be seen in such a place as a public skating rink. But the spirited sister defied the warning and went skating in fancy dress, hoping her disguise as a musical comedy character, the Chocolate Soldier, would cover her illicit leisure-time pursuit. Unfortunately, she was photographed and identified in a subsequent picture printed in the local newspaper. She was sacked instantaneously.

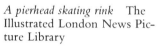

A pierhead skating rink The Illustrated London News Picture Library

Apprentices aspiring to be showroom girls came from what were considered to be 'good homes'. They were chosen with considerable care, often on family recommendations, and given training in elocution, deportment, and manners. These young women, some just children, entered a stratified community. The hierarchy of stores involved a pecking order.

Selling was the province of the first, second, third, and fourth hands, the showroom assistants who carried 'books' to record customers' purchases, made either on account or for cash, upon which were based the commission (1½d. to 3d. per pound). Their books were collected up each day by the counting house. These showroom hands were helped by the apprentices, who packed goods, found chairs for madam, ran errands and did the daily chores, such as 'dressing out' counters and display cabinets or dusting, before the day's business began.

The apprentices were hierarchical, too, for the top apprentice was allowed to hold a book, but subject to the supervision and counter signatures of a showroom assistant. Two other classes of girls were employed – workroom assistants and the shop girls. The latter were not the same as the apprenticed showroom girls and mixing was discouraged between those holding indentures and the ordinary shop girls.

Above everyone were the buyers, with the men dressed in morning suits and striped trousers. Female buyers wore stunning gowns made of silk moiré with satin trains to demonstrate their status. Buyers had power to sack at a moment's displeasure, but staff took care not to incur their wrath. In practice, buyers were often generous in their help towards apprentices, remembering, perhaps, their own days under indentures. The atmosphere within stores was not one of repression and resentment, rather a studied courtesy to each other and effortless acceptance of relative positions. Good manners and behaviour pervaded the stores.

Store keeping was a model of gentle service. Customers received complete attention as assistant and apprentices discreetly dealt with their requirements. The approach of a customer would see the first hand moving in and, when another appeared, the second hand would move to station. If a junior hand met some difficulty, there would be a flick of an eyebrow from him to a senior, who, in unspoken ritual, quickly moved over to deal with the matter. Unbeknown to account customers, an apprentice might move off at a nod to call the counting house to check a customer's standing and debts. This was very necessary when the stores operated what were known as 'appro' books.

At Folkestone, for example, the Plummer sales staff had pink approbation books as well as their standard sales pads. These were for recording requests from any customers who wanted a selection of items to be sent to their homes on approval. Delivery vans were packed with pine boxes, carried by thick leather straps, into which the stores had placed merchandise wrapped in yards of tissue paper. After inspection at home, the customer returned items not required.

Buyers controlled the price tickets for merchandise. The more expensive lines, such as 'exclusive' model gowns, were kept in special glass cases and prices were only quoted on request. A garment might be placed in the windows facing on to the street but not marked with a price like other items

*'The Mode of the Moment' –
black taffeta hat trimmed with
ospreys, from Debenham &
Freebody* The Illustrated London News Picture Library

on display. This indicated an exclusive line. Suitings for women were a
major exercise in personal service. Fitters were called down from workrooms, pin cushions strapped to their wrists as they measured and fitted
customers. Miles of Donegal and Harris Tweeds, or West of England Flannel – fabrics noted for their 'hang' and 'curving to the figure' – were sold.
Corsets with front and back lacing were cut and fitted by experts, sometimes
to medical prescription.

Underwear came in georgette, crêpe de chine, tafetta, and silk moiré.
Cotton was considered a cheap material. Juvenile departments specialized in
uniforms for private schools, made from the best materials. Better class
stores left the supply of common children's smocks, the everyday wear of
working-class school children and often washed each night, to the more
popular shops.

Buyers from provincial department stores regularly visited London and
the big fashion exhibitions to keep abreast of fashion trends. They placed
their orders not only with visiting travellers but also liked to go personally to
wholesalers such as Debenham & Freebody's City business house.

'The gowns were simply stunning, really breathtaking,' recalled Mrs Cotton, who at 20 was probably one of the youngest buyers in the pre-war
history of department stores. 'We had to be careful not to be carried away by
the splendour of the garments and the surroundings. The buyer had a
budget. A Debenhams' label was a mark of the highest quality and, like
everyone, I delighted in the D & F catalogues, or the chance to examine what
was on offer. Some of the most gorgeous fabrics and dresses I have ever seen
came from Debenham & Freebody.'

83

In London, Selfridges, Harrods and Whiteleys were unsure of their future role and prospects. Many asked whether their era would pass. Two businesses which needed the security of better capitalized owners were Marshall & Snelgrove, and Harvey Nichols in Knightsbridge. There was strong inflation and the cost of living in 1919 was 125 per cent higher than six years before. Unions were pressing for better representation and minimum wages at Harvey Nichols.

Debenhams needed capital, too, yet was in a better position to raise funds than Marshall & Snelgrove, with which it had worked through the war years. The answer was a merger, followed by an enlargement of capital.

The rationale for the merger was explained succinctly by Ernest Debenham in March 1919. He said:

Speaking for myself, it had always been one of my ambitions that our business and Marshall's should cease to be rivals and agree to work together. It has always appeared to me that competition between us was wasteful and useless. We touched one another as regards premises; we both had the necessity of looking ahead and acquiring premises adjoining our own, for our future development.

It was therefore obviously undesirable that we should compete with one another in this direction. Then it was evident that, of all the businesses in London, this was the one we could look forward to working with with most hope of success. It was a business with nearly as old traditions as our own, and it had always been conducted in the same honourable manner. It had treated its staff in the same way that we had treated ours, and the staff compared very favourably with our own. Beyond this again, the class of business and the *clientèle* with which Marshall's dealt was very much the same as our own. This perhaps was the most important feature which led us to come to a working agreement with them, because the one fixed policy of these businesses is that we shall keep up the quality of our trade.

Edward Marshall strongly recommended the terms of the merger via Textile Securities to shareholders, to whom the idea already seemed inevitable.

Across in Knightsbridge, Harvey Nichols, with annual profits of only £37 000, saw a similar link-up with Debenhams as an answer to fierce competition from neighbouring areas. Capital, it seemed, could be raised by big groups. Debenhams' profits were now averaging £365 000 a year. There were wartime bank loans to repay and post-war modernization to be financed.

Talks began late in 1919 with Debenhams, which liked the idea of a big stake in Knightsbridge. The 80-year-old Harvey Nichols offered valuable freehold premises, and a trade capable of reform with the same Debenham skills which had saved Marshall & Snelgrove from decline. By December, Ernest Debenham as chairman and Oliver were running two managing directors in harness, James Spence and Frederick Richmond, and the small team of four paid over £217 040 in cash plus a handsome block of Preference shares for full ownership of the Knightsbridge enterprise, whose property and fittings were valued alone at £304 000.

Negotiations to buy up Harvey Nichols were among the last major decisions of Frederick Oliver as joint managing director, for in March 1920, blaming his health, he surrendered managerial functions to become a deputy chairman. Oliver was rich and held in high esteem, but he wished to write a monumental work on politics before his health failed him. His access to high places was undiminished. Harvey Nichols seemed a deal not out of tune with the times. Like Marshall & Snelgrove, Harvey Nichols had a considerable indebtedness to Debenham & Freebody's wholesaling business.

This deal, however, drained Debenhams' reserves of capital and by the following summer of 1920 it was back in the City markets seeking yet more finance from the public and investment institutions. Profits of Debenhams, Marshall & Snelgrove and Harvey Nichols now amounted to a combined £1 150 000. Eager for expansion, Debenhams bought, before raising new capital, J. & E. Bumpus, the book business. It came back for even more funds in 1921. Exports in 1919 had risen by 30 per cent, and the mood was expansive, perhaps optimistic, given the slow recovery from warfare by retailers.

Oliver's eye for a good deal can be seen in property records. He had bought for Debenhams Marylebone's Old Town Hall (a newly built replacement was commandeered in the Great War by the Ministry of Pensions) for just £26 000.

Amalgamations in retail drapery were the order of the day. Harrods had taken over Dickins & Jones in Regent Street. Just as startling was Barkers' acquisition of Derry & Toms, its neighbour, to create a trading area of 2½ acres. Barkers had already swallowed Pontings, and Kensington became a magnet for custom from people moving into the fast developing estates of South London.

The purchase of Harvey Nichols gave Debenhams a full-blooded stake in Knightsbridge's rival and slightly up-market shopping area, and Barkers had moved fast to head off a bid for Derry & Toms. After all Debenhams had fused with Marshall & Snelgrove the previous year, and here it was buying Harvey Nichols and known to be interested in Barkers' neighbour.

Headlines came to Debenhams in an unexpected way in July 1921. It had long run approved benevolent societies for staff welfare purposes and a revaluation of investments yielded a surplus. With this money, the company, with 1500 employees, decided to pioneer a dental service at low cost, free to some. Bad teeth mean bad health and bad health means bad business, declared A. Debenham Sweeting, the staff societies' secretary in press interviews. It was probably the first staff dental service in Britain and hundreds of employees regularly paraded in the evenings before dentists.

A school for employees, approved by the London County Council, had also started up, in the wake of the Fisher *Education Act*. Two-thirds of the Debenhams staff came from elementary schools and one-third from other secondary schools. Ernest Debenham enlisted officers of the then Shop Assistants' Union to interest his staff in further education (500 young people attended a meeting in January 1920 to hear their chairman and union leaders explain the merits of education). Debenhams also sent females to the working women's colleges.

More down to earth was the new practice of conducting New Year sales to clear stocks of unsold goods. The transformation of London's most famous houses, as the big department stores liked to call themselves, was a means of

85

The sales in 1910   Radio Times
Hulton Picture Library

rationalizing stock quickly rather than a deliberate concession to the mas
markets developing elsewhere. Yet it was a rare opportunity for people o
lower incomes to purchase goods bearing the labels of the big name Londo
stores. Just how the sales were received by the public can be divined in som
contemporary descriptions:

Pall Mall Gazette December 31, 1920:

HUNTING IN THE WEST END
WOMEN EARLY ON THE WARPATH
UNDISMAYED
RAIN NO DETERRENT TO BARGAIN SEEKERS
(BY A MERE MAN.)

Was there a woman dismayed this morning when the rain pattered on the windo
pane and the pavements revealed themselves as small muddy lakes, with only he
and there a comparatively clean spot?

Apparently not. With serviceable rainproof or pull-on hats, stout shoes—of the
stockings I say nothing!—and mackintoshes of every hue, they were to be seen i
Tube trains and emerging from railway termini.

Most of them were umbrellaless—for, as one of them explained, both hands a
needed for bargain counters—but had their vanity bags slung over their arms, an
sale catalogues protruding therefrom.

Some of the middle-aged women were speaking with horror of the days whe
skirts were long and rainy days a misery. Now, apparently, they don't matter—no
at least, while on every hand bargains are waiting to be snapped up.

Morning Post January 3, 1921:

Messrs. Debenham and Freebody, of Wigmore-street, off Oxford-street, ope
their sale this morning, and it will last until Saturday week. They offer furs and silk
at half-price, and tempting bargains in many other departments. They announce tha

86

owing to the recent fall in the prices of raw skins they will offer practically their whole stock of fur coats, stoles, and muffs at a reduction of 50 per cent, in order to clear their shelves and make room for more. They state explicitly that no goods have been purchased specially for the sale. Among other special bargains are tailor suits for the early spring, blouses in hues of ivory, champagne, flesh, lemon, rust, and a variety of other shades; ladies underwear, and a large stock of silks at half price.

Messrs. MARSHALL and SNELGROVE, of Vere-street and Oxford-street, open a three weeks' sale to-day. They, also, are clearing out their fur coats and wraps at half the prices marked a week ago, and similar reductions are made in Lyons tinsel brocades, brocade silks, fancy velvets, and printed ninons. Other bargains are in early spring suits for women, model coats and skirts, stockinette coat frocks, restaurant and evening frocks, blankets, underclothing, petticoats of new design, children's clothes, mushroom sailor hats, ribbons, and handkerchiefs.

Messrs. HARVEY NICHOLS and Co. (Limited) of Knightsbridge, whose sale, beginning this morning, will last for three weeks, make some general observations on the economic situation in their catalogue. 'No one (they say) would welcome a return to normal prices more than ourselves, but we are afraid this is impossible for a good many years to come. In any case, we shall offer during the sale the whole of our stock at prices which will be as low as, and in all probability much lower than, those that are likely to obtain during the forthcoming year.' Like some other houses, they are offering a large selection of expensive furs at half price. Other attractions are in tailored suits, wrap cloaks, country skirts, evening dresses, fashionable hats, sports coats and suits, and Indian carpets.

Westminster Gazette, January 4, 1921:

THE SALES
A WOMAN'S VIEW OF THE POSITION
(By a Lady Correspondent.)

Piqued, and perhaps stimulated by the accounts I had read of congestion at the sales, and of bargains such as one has only encountered in dreams these later years, I set out on my mission of going round the shops yesterday.

As the day progressed, an early suspicion grew into certainty. All these sensational accounts I had read must have been written by men—simple creatures who had never explored the West End in the full tide of the opening sales. Crowds there were, of course, but such crowds as daunt no feminine heart. One could buy, if not exactly at leisure, at any rate without a larger amount of inconvenience than is usual at such times. As for the bargains, there were certainly goods at prices lower than have been seen for two or three years, but nobody was amazed. This was what every woman had been expecting. And, apart from furs, which seem to have plunged downward in price, the significant reductions were in the cheaper articles of clothing and in those made-up goods which must be disposed of now or miss their market. Better articles still command a price, although the keen buyer can see that even these are cheaper than they were.

My round began with Messrs. Debenham and Freebody's, and it was a happy choice, as giving the characteristic note of the day, for here was a wonderful stock of furs, and every garment could be had at one-half the marked price, whether it was a seal-musquash coat at 495 guineas, or an opossum stole at 8 guineas. Furs have experienced a sensational drop in price at the sales of skins, but these will only be coming on the market some months hence, and it is in anticipation of what must then happen that Messrs. Debenham and Freebody have taken time by the forelock. So, too, with rich silks, among which are really beautiful fabrics. Many can be had for half the marked price, and a stock which is valued at £40 000 affords the widest

range of choice. Shoes of all kinds offer as remarkable an opportunity, especiall`
when one has dark hints from the 'buyers' that footwear may shortly be even highe`
in price than hitherto.

Turning into Messrs. Marshall and Snelgrove's one catches again the real breath`
lessness of the sale atmosphere. There is such a number of departments that unles`
one comes with some preconceived notions, one is lost amid the bewildering variet`
of temptations. But yesterday most of the shoppers must have had their minds mad`
up, for apart from the furs and silks, one found the greater congestion round th`
tea-gowns, the blouses, and the sports coats—a name that now covers a quit`
extraordinary series of wraps available for almost all outdoor occasions. There was`
briskness, too, in the departments for blankets and household linens, suggestive c`
the desire of the housewife to replenish those linen cupboards which have bee`
rather neglected during years of war, and of the high prices that war brings.

These descriptions are familiar, if more than 50 years old. The annual specta`
cle is an event newspapers never tire of covering. Shoplifting was rife in th`
1920s and magistrates' records indicate that many people of wealth anc`
position were tempted to steal. Debenhams prosecuted without fear o`
favour. Indeed it came down with a Victorian harshness on the mos`
privileged offenders, guilty of dishonesty and disgracing their positions ir
society.

There was the same rigour in dealing with customers who fell on bac`
times and ran up debts. Liquidations were often initiated to ensure no slack`
ness among those with whom it dealt. The 'rag trade' knew Debenhams t`
be harsh, though always helpful to newcomers with ideas who had initia`
working capital problems. Once helped, a small supplier was expected t`
deliver and to act with prudence in dealing with the store group.

Some evidence exists of discretion in the case of long-standing customer`
holding accounts at big stores. More than a few people apparently of consid`
erable status were helped in the twenties.

Less fortunate, however, was a leading actress, Constance Collier, whon`
Debenhams took to Bloomsbury County Court for non-payment fo`
flowers valued at £16. 9s. 3d. delivered to the Savoy Theatre. Miss Collier`
though her maid regularly ordered flowers by telephone, denied this particu`
lar order. Miss Collier apparently captivated Judge Bray, hearing the evi`
dence. When Debenhams' prosecutor, Mr R. J. White, declared he did no`
wish to ask any more questions of the actress, the Judge solemnly remarked`
'It looks as if I am the only one who would like to see Miss Collier again.`
The actress won the case and Debenhams, seeming to lack humour bu`
concerned for its prosecuting record, sought unsuccessfully to appeal. Eng`
land smiled.

Unbeknown to customers at major stores, there existed a semi-secre`
system of weeding out customers who were 'a bad lot'. The big store owner`
had for over a century built up the Mutual Communication Society. Thi`
organization had started in a London coffee house to discuss debtors, an`
problems with defaulters. Weekly meetings were being held in 1920.

Gathered in the Connaught Rooms, London, for their 113th dinner on 2`
November, they received a report on developments. Mr A. E. W. Coope`

CHILDREN'S DAINTY CLOTHES

Our Children's Outfitting Department is one of the most interesting sections of our business, and has gained what we believe to be a well-deserved reputation for the dainty and exclusive character of its productions. Every garment is designed by our own expert, and the materials used are thoroughly practical and reliable.

DAINTY FROCK (as sketch), entirely hand sewn, of ivory spot net over slip of ivory ninon, with bodice of taffeta, in shades of pink or blue.

Size for 2 years.	Price	79/6
,, ,, 3 ,,	,,	84/-
,, ,, 4 ,,	,,	89/6
,, ,, 5 ,,	,,	95/-

This model can be copied in plain net if desired.

LAYETTES.

We have always in stock a wonderful variety of Infants' Garments. Short Coating Outfits, Cots and Baskets, all exclusive in design and made from the best quality materials. Illustrated catalogue post free.

Debenham & Freebody
(DEBENHAM'S LIMITED)
Wigmore Street.
(Cavendish Square) London. W1

RELIABLE AND DISTINCTIVE FURS

at *Extremely Moderate Prices.*

Made from specially selected skins in the most becoming shapes and worked by high-class skilled furriers.

Beautiful Natural Skunk Collar Shape, cut on entirely new lines, giving great warmth and comfort, made of best quality skins, perfectly worked **25 Gns.**

6-skins natural skunk muff, excellent quality **11 Gns.**

FUR RENOVATIONS.

Customers requiring their Furs remodelled or renovated are strongly advised to put them in hand at once and thus save the disappointment of having to wait when the colder weather comes. The latest shapes and models for this season are now to be seen in our Salon. Minute attention is given to this section, and every alteration is executed by skilled workmen at most moderate prices

Harvey Nichols of Knightsbridge
., Knightsbridge, London, S.W.1.

INEXPENSIVE JAPANESE PURE SILK NIGHTGOWN

WE have now in stock a large variety of Nightgowns in new and exclusive shapes, specially designed and made in our own workrooms from materials of exceptional value and quality.

Useful NIGHTGOWN made in good quality Jap Silk, trimmed with folds of material and design of hand embroidery.

Price 21/9

Also in Crêpe-de-Chine in pale shades .. 29/6

MARSHALL & SNELGROVE
VERE·STREET·AND·OXFORD·STREET
LONDON·W1

Sent on Approval.

Advertisements in The Sketch, *1921* The Illustrated London News Picture Library

declared that the society had been in existence for more than 100 years which was a very fine record. It was clear that when the first members used to meet in a coffee shop they had the same troubles in regard to obtaining payment of accounts. The idea of the society, he continued, was reciprocity and he thought his firm (Selfridge & Co.) had done their part in reciprocating since they were admitted to membership. There was never a time when such a society was more important. A few months ago people were supposed to be worth a certain amount and they were on paper, but today they were not worth half as much. The society could, and did, render quite a lot of assistance, and it should be supported to the fullest possible extent.

Another revealed 100 000 ordering inquiries went through to the society' central office. In the period January to November there had been a rise of 2000 in 'special' inquiries. Agents throughout England, Scotland and Ireland (not Wales) undertook debt inquiries in return for subscriptions to the MCS A central register of information blacklisted certain people, particularly passers of bad cheques and people placing fraudulent overseas orders.

A need for tighter control of credit was seen as vital. Profits were getting harder to earn. The recovery from the Great War was short-lived for Debenhams. In 1921 as a consequence of falling prices and difficult exchange the company had orders cancelled and goods refused by their overseas customers to the amount of about £750 000. They had not only lost the profit they would have made on this amount, but had had to write down to their market value the goods returned.

Presiding at the annual meeting Ernest Debenham said the past year had been a very difficult one for trade. In the first half-year they had increased their business by nearly 40 per cent, and they started the second half-year with very large orders in hand, but immediately after the coal strike in October business became increasingly bad, money became increasingly dear and the wise and prudent policy of the Government in reducing its debt could not be effected without taking so much from the pockets of the taxpayers.

As a consequence, the purchasing power of the public was seriously diminished, and that was further affected by Britain's foreign exchange problems. Large foreign orders had to be cancelled. The firm stood in a very strong financial position. As to the current year, it was difficult to prophesy but it could hardly fail to be a very lean one.

During the last seven years the company had increased its business four and a half times, and had obtained a large and increasing volume of foreign trade. The main source of their anxiety was that all overseas trade had fallen under a cloud, and he saw no signs of the cloud lifting in the immediate future.

Britain was clearly experiencing an end to the post-war boom. Men over 21 and women over 30 with fixed addresses now had the vote, but, in the land fit for heroes, too many workers began to use pawn shops. Unemployment in 1921 reached 2 000 000 and trouble broke out everywhere particularly in the coal mines which had been nationalized for war purposes but were subsequently returned to private ownership amid a bitter strike Within a few years, a Labour Government took office for the first time, yet

Marshall & Snelgrove tailor-mades worn by Miss Molly Ramsden
The Illustrated London News Picture Library

the administration, formed in 1924, proved short-lived – a sad time for the pioneers who, years before, had gathered in Laycock's Cafe, at the back of Busby's noted store in Bradford, a cradle of the old Independent Labour Party.

The mergers between Debenham & Freebody and the Marshall & Snelgrove and Harvey Nichols stores were not the only talk of the drapery and department store world. For some time there had been rumours of acquisitions and complicated share investments in provincial businesses by a certain City financier emerging from the disastrous failure of the Commercial Bank of London. He was Clarence Charles Hatry, who indulged expensive tastes, had begun business life as an insurance broker, and apparently made money with ease. Hatry had a yacht and one of his racehorses, Furious, won the Lincolnshire Handicap in 1920. He was responsible for the flotation of British Glass Industries, an over-capitalized company which also met with disaster, and he was later involved in mergers within the steel industry, finally ending up in prison having dishonoured the City's reputation through frauds of another creation, the Austin Friars Trust.

Hatry was to prove dishonest, but, undaunted by early setbacks in his ambitious manipulation of stock, he can, nonetheless, be said to have created the foundations for the modern nationwide Debenhams department store group. His interest in shopkeeping was not without inside knowledge, for he was the son of a Hampstead silk merchant. In a whirlwind of deals, he toured the provinces, making tempting offers to families who owned and controlled well-sited stores but in the post-armistice years lacked the resources to refurbish them or lacked management skills. Some stores he acquired outright and others were tempted by initial share purchases. In a few cases he selected some bright stores, such as Bon Marché at Gloucester, where there was management talent to be utilized within the group he envisaged.

There were many suspicions about Hatry, one of the first asset strippers, but a man with an ability to see a case for amalgamations to obtain benefits of more uniform management policies and coordinated buying of goods. The stores had freehold properties in attractive town centre sites which might be sold or redeveloped, and Hatry frequently increased the temptation of his many offers by not insisting that existing owners and their families should leave the business. As he put it, he was investing in what he called a Drapery Trust, which would provide new working capital and ideas.

Concentration and combinations in retailing were something new, although rationalization and mergers had become familiar in the early 1920s. The creation of Distillers, Imperial Chemical Industries, United Alkali, the British Dyestuffs Corporation, and British Match were a few examples. A long-established free trade tradition had been disrupted by protectionism and the future was seen, in highly competitive conditions with poor profit margins, to rest with the conglomeration and outright mergers. Hatry found ready listeners during his trips to see candidates for his new Drapery Trust.

In London, Debenhams kept a wary eye on any news about Hatry. One day the upstart young man might come calling.

5 Wheeling and dealing

The first prerequisite for recovery should be by enlargement of the unit 'both by growth and the regrouping of units through consolidation or other forms of association, so as to obtain the full benefits of large scale production, elimination of waste, standardization, and simplification of practice.

House of Commons Committee on *Industry and Trade*, 1928-29.

On 7 March 1925 a Mr Alfred Spicer and his son Herbert sat in the offices of Curl Brothers, Norwich, and signed an agreement under which the father paid the East Anglian firm £40 in return for the opportunity of the son to learn the drapery trade in the next three years at a salary of £26 a year plus board and lodging 'and all other necessaries'. Herbert Spencer Spicer was about to begin a career in retailing and it cost 2s. 6d. to seal the indenture.

Before the year was out the young Spicer was to be employed within an empire nominally headed by the Marquess of Winchester, chairman of the Victoria Falls and Transvaal Power Company, but in reality an investment trust created by the paperwork and intrigues of Clarence Hatry, through his Austin Friars Investment Trust.

Spicer was just one of many hundreds of young people setting out on a career in retailing at a time when the idea of amalgamations among companies and family-run businesses had begun to gain currency. The merits of large-scale enterprise within manufacturing were the subject of considerable advocacy by politicians and industrialists. Some of this enthusiasm communicated itself to shopkeepers, particularly those lacking working capital and operating on credit. In reality, it meant the big concern got bigger and the smaller struggling enterprise had to surrender its once cherished independence.

During 1926, H. Gordon Selfridge and his son, Harry G. Selfridge Jnr, put together the Gordon Selfridge Trust and formed Selfridge Provincial Stores. It was an impressive grouping, comprising Jones Bros and John Barnes of London; George Henry Lee, Liverpool; Cole Bros, Sheffield; Bull, Reading; Brown Thomas & Co., Dublin; Blinkhorn, Gloucester; C. J. Hardy, Leeds; Caleys, Windsor; Brice & Son, Northampton; Needham & Sons, Brighton; Trewin Bros, Watford; Thomson's, Peterborough; and Dorell, St Albans.

Selfridge's founder, Harry Senior, pronounced his conviction that the profit-earning capacity of these provincial interests 'is not less than that of Selfridge's London'.

93

What became clear during that year was that Selfridge was not alone in touring provincial centres to plan a new grouping of interests. He raced to obtain control of other businesses, including South London stores such as Bon Marché, and Quin & Axtens of Brixton, Holdron's of Peckham, and Pratt's of Streatham. By April 1927, Selfridges linked up with Whiteleys. In the race was a certain Sir Arthur Wheeler, who promoted the formation of United Drapery Stores from seven stores (Hawes Bros, Hinds & Co., Blundell, Carton & Co., Shinners, Walker & Penistans, and Young) from Clapham to Sevenoaks, later adding the ill-fated Glave's in the West End.

The activity drew from the *Drapers' Record* a prediction:

The formation of big trusts, combines and fusions is certain to entail changes in trade methods and customs. There will be attempts to modify or alter some of the recognized rules of the trade, and unified control is bound to mean the elimination of a certain amount of individuality.

It was a remark that must have drawn assent from James Marshall, who died in 1926 as the epoch of combination began with this frenzy of stock market promotions and take-over deals within retailing. Nonetheless, his beloved Marshall & Snelgrove might have been likened to a giant whale beached by the changing tides of trade.

A few days before Christmas 1925, City investors had received a prospectus outlining the creation of the Drapery and General Investment Trust. They were asked to subscribe £2m for shares in a new enterprise to carry on the business of drapery and department stores. Behind the scenes, long negotiations had taken place with the owners of Curls of Norwich and seven other long established businesses, Dawson Brothers (1848), H. C. Russell (1864), and Staddons (1870) from London, Kennards of Croydon (1853) Marshall (a strong Yorkshire group spun off from Marshall & Snelgrove and founded in 1843), Pettigrew & Stephens of Glasgow (1888) and the South Coast stores group Plummer Roddis (1887).

This was a conglomerate of businesses in which Clarence Hatry had built up a succession of interests and his Austin Friars Trust got nearly £1.8m from the new Drapery Trust for the transfer of interests under a bewildering series of separate deals, contracts and understandings. Huge compensation fortunes and handsome service contracts were made with the flotation of the new Drapery Trust.

By the autumn of 1926, Debenhams was feeling the effects of economic difficulties. The marked progress and recovery from war was checked. Owing to the General Strike and the coal strike, Ernest Debenham saw profits falling for the year well below the average for the previous four. Frederick Oliver, as deputy chairman, said he wanted to retire to write his book while his health allowed. With advice from the Whitehall Trust, it was decided to form Debenham Securities Ltd to buy the whole of the Ordinary shares to ensure a continuity of management while providing a means for buying out the Oliver interests.

Under the deal, two Olivers, Mark and John Scott, received £750 000 in cash from the new Debenham Securities. Ernest Debenham took £218 324 in cash plus nearly 1.3m Ordinary shares in the new concern. Another be

94

neficiary was F. Richmond (£303 743 and over 400 000 shares). And big sums of cash went to J. Spence (nearly £70 000), G. M. Wright (£99 076), and C. J. L. Snowden (£40 071). These were truly fortunes at the date of the various agreements.

Ernest now became chairman of the new Debenham Securities, which raised public money to finance the rearrangement of shareholdings. The directors were George Maurice Wright, a brilliant accountant, James Spence, an expert trader, Frederick Richmond, and Piers K. Debenham, plus a banker William Paine. Wright and Richmond were future chairmen of the shops group.

Meanwhile, Clarence Hatry was still stalking the provinces, yet to arrive in the Debenhams boardroom with a grand design.

Hatry had great ambitions. Fortunes could be built by stock manipulation and department stores were a good hunting ground for the preying Hatry. Families concerned for their investment in stores, with many ageing premises needing refurbishment and an injection of buying skills appropriate to a population now looking for value as well as quality, were willing to listen when Hatry or his associates came calling.

An obvious target was Selincourt & Sons, incorporated at the end of the Great War, but built up by Charles De Selincourt from its beginnings more than sixty years before as warehousemen, manufacturers of costumes, mantles, coats and cloaks and well known silk merchants and furriers. Incorporation was to be followed by a slide in profits, and the acquisition of several

rwick House

Top: *Handleys of Southsea*

Above: *Spooners' trade card, showing their first delivery van*

Right: *Spooners of Plymouth on fire, 1902*

other businesses could not by 1925 restore profits even to the levels of war years. Heir to the business, Martin De Selincourt reached an agreement in June 1926 with Hatry by which the family firm would go into the Drapery Trust. Money was raised with a stock issue, and at the same time Stagg & Russell went to the stock markets.

The wheeling and dealing became even dizzier by 1927, while the rival Debenhams, blissfully watching at a distance, was more concerned with setting up a staff golfing society based on Sonning Golf Club, then owned by three directors Frederick Richmond, G. Maurice Wright, and Ernest Cutts (the last name was brought in with Harvey Nichols).

By 6 January 1927, Hatry's complex negotiations reached a climax. The Drapery Trust, with direct interests or holdings, now controlled Frank Drury of Manchester (1912), Margaret Marks of Knightsbridge (1923), and Warwick House, a successor to Hollidays of Birmingham (1836). More public finance was sought for agreements to take interests in six major provincial enterprises, the biggest being the concern of Bobby & Co., with stores from Margate to Exeter and Torquay, and from High Wycombe to Leamington Spa.

The others were the well managed Bon Marché of Gloucester, run by J. R. Pope & Sons, Footman Pretty & Co. of Ipswich, Handleys of Southsea, Jones & Co. of Bristol, Wellsteeds of Reading, Edwin Jones of Southampton, Spooners of Plymouth, and Smiths of Stratford on Avon.

To add to the complexities, a deal was also struck with the associated Scottish Drapery Corporation, which also issued a share prospectus. Scotland contributed Patrick Thompson (Edinburgh), D. M. Brown (Dundee) and Watt & Grant (Aberdeen).

A massive national group of drapers and department stores had been put together with bewildering speed in just a few years. Profits were around £600 000. Hatry had sold to the public and to scores of highly individual store operators the idea of pooling their know-how in difficult times, for 1926 was the year of the General Strike, massive unrest and fears for future security.

Huddled together amid depressed trading conditions such businesses were a group with 11 000 employees in sixty-five stores hoping to derive mutual security and growth through lean years. Amalgamations were an answer to multiples and the cooperatives, which had begun to take prime sites and to compete hard on both credit and ready cash terms, biting into the limited spending power of people concerned with necessities. Hatry seemed a saviour. Whatever else he did around this time, which brought him disgrace and prison, his ideas were certainly perceptive.

It might cause tongue-biting in Debenhams today to learn that in 1927 the Drapery Trust announced:

A department has been started for the purpose of developing a system of centralized cooperative buying from which it is anticipated that a considerable income will in [the] course of time be derived for the company and its subsidiaries.

The Drapery Trust now boasted 18m recorded transactions a year, with a spread of interests over every class of the drapery trade, and, needing a West

97

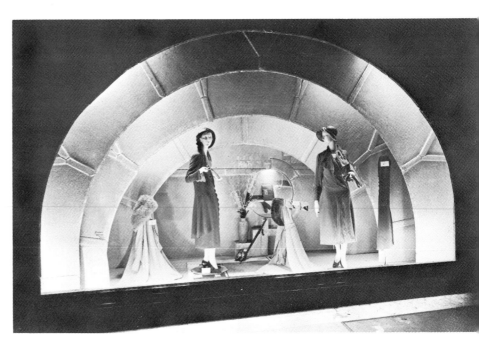

Window display in the new Swan & Edgar building

End 'flagship' it now brought in Swan & Edgar, with its majestic new premises. Around the country, the general shopping public was blissfully unaware that ownership of its favourite drapers and general departmental stores had been changing hands.

The men at the Drapery Trust were often both directors of the parent company and fully responsible for subsidiaries trading under traditional names. Individuality of established shops was carefully preserved by retaining a continuity of management. The Trust's business philosophy was, however, far sighted and well worth recording. As set down in a brochure sent to shareholders, it was:

A Wider and keener buying by reason of combined purchasing power. Thus better values are offered to the public and trade developed on the sound basis of lowest selling prices.

B The pooling of technical knowledge and service for the benefit of the various businesses.

C The employment of experts in various branches of the trade whose services could not be afforded by the individual businesses.

D The attraction to ambitious staffs of both sexes to seek employment in the Drapery Trust establishments because of the wider scope for advancement.

E The financial facilities afforded to individual businesses to take advantage of favourable opportunities for expansion.

That year of 1927 saw Lindbergh flying the Atlantic, an event which stirred the imagination of a public sadly in need of heroes. In the City, Hatry

98

was admired by investors disturbed by the insecurity occasioned when Britain, deep in debt, had in 1925 come off the gold standard. The coal industry was drifting into decline and losses, and even Beaverbrook advocated Hatry-style combination to save the mines. People everywhere were hard up and the advent of popular picture houses showing films for a few pennies' admission were the places where mass shoppers found amusement, rather than in the theatres where those still able to dress up maintained their social presence with Debenhams' evening wear.

People struggled to maintain their children in new schools and adult education was burgeoning everywhere, often rooted in semi-political organizations determined to rear future leaders as well as satisfy a hunger for knowledge to understand a society that still had deep divisions. Yet Baldwin was preaching stability as envisaged by Bonar Law. It contrasted sharply with the mercurial years of Lloyd George or the thoughtful times of Balfour. Attitudes towards the providers of capital and businessmen were, in general, best described as suspicious.

The national hunger was for work, an expanding economy, and incomes to buy all the goods and services offered by Hatry's stores, where, through the many products, could be gleaned insights into the world of others still able to afford them. Manufacturers of consumer goods wanted markets.

It is not fanciful to guess how all this had made its impact on Debenham's former deputy chairman, Frederick Oliver, champion of the ordinary man's wish for a better way and a more rewarding economic system. He was a late Victorian who now argued passionately in his writing, but his personal influence had declined since he had helped unseat Asquith. The epoch of the take-over bid, the big City deal, and better capitalized competition had arrived. Struggles for power were now commonplace. This was not the time for gentlemen and orderly negotiation.

Debenhams experienced a taste of things to come in business when it lost a struggle with Swears & Wells to regain control in 1928 of Cavendish House in Cheltenham, which in 1888 had been allowed to go its own way by Freebody. Men settled for money offered by others, not the future logic of association proposed by Debenhams in its unfortunate efforts to re-enter Cheltenham.

The 'Great Slump' of 1928 gave the successors to the Debenham and Oliver families the means of securing for the original firm, now enlarged by Marshall & Snelgrove and Harvey Nichols, a combination in the British retail trade beyond even the now departed Oliver's expansionist ideas of the early 1900s.

In the higher echelons of society, argument raged about Free Trade, the Empire's role, and the chronic depression. In the Lancashire cotton industry some 238 mills changed hands between 1919 and 1920. Some 12 per cent of the working population, which was growing relentlessly, were unemployed in 1928. This was a pendulum year when horse-drawn vehicles lived alongside cars, now arriving by the thousands on the roads of Britain.

The Central Electricity Board was two years old, and national broadcasting but six years old. In May 1928, there were 2½m radio receiving sets, and Debenhams had provided six pairs of earphones in its library at Chapel

Place, London, so a few employees could listen to concerts during their breaks from work.

For the staff there had been changes in the rules of the Debenham's Workers Approved Society, which protected the sick employee. Members with two years' company service were now guaranteed full wages for the first six weeks of illness and half pay for the second six weeks. Thereafter, they would be on state benefits only. Staff provisions included help toward membership of the Hospital Savings Association. Outings were organized to theatres – in 1928 a party saw Charles Laughton in *Alibi* by Agatha Christie. Staff libraries were busy places, too. Children of distressed employees were financed for education at the Purley Trade Schools.

The restraint of the London businesses is caught in a note sent to the Oxford Street staff from the staff at the City House, centre of the wholesaling operations:

'The Gentlemen of St Paul's wish to try their skill at a game of cricket with the Gentlemen of the West. If the invitation is accepted the Gentlemen of St Paul's will be glad of an early reply.' Lazy days at the Eastcote sports ground led to friendships across the boundaries of individual businesses.

Employees developed a kind of wry humour and loyalty to their own stores, to carry them through the day. They would talk about glove fights (a reference to any woman insisting on getting a 7¼ hand into a 6½ pair of gloves), camouflage sales (a reference to a hosiery purchase by a woman with poor legs), and defeating form (a troublesome customer for corsetry). One store wit described gowns as clothes made for modern Eves from leaves plucked from Adam's bank book. Veils were articles to cover complexions that did not exist. The manicure department was described as a section which held hands for a profit. In February 1927, some workers who could be found grumbling were those who had joined the Debenhams Special Constabulary, for the Commissioner of Metropolitan Police refused them permission to go to Paris for an Easter outing he felt would 'not be advisable'.

There was fun, within limits, in even the most formal emporium. At Harvey Nichols, during the opening in 1934 of new furniture salons, staff had difficulty retaining their composure, when four trumpeters were deployed in the centre of the Lift Hall heralding – and deafening – each of the first customers and guests. Also in 1927 fire protection devices went haywire and flooded Harvey Nichols' premises in Knightsbridge. A contributor to the Debenhams' staff journal, *Mayfair One*, describing the 'mounting water' and an SOS for help from other stores, wrote: 'Surely our friends at Debenhams would pause in the midst of buying up more businesses to send aid to their loyal ship Harvey Nichols?'

Clearly the staff felt, even in humour, that management was becoming very concerned with take-overs. And something big was in the winds of 1927.

On 18 November 1927, Clarence Hatry scrawled his signature across a sixpenny stamp affixed to the bottom of a neatly typed contractual letter addressed to G. M. Wright at Debenham Securities from Hatry's Austin Friars Trust. This act sealed a scheme whereby Debenhams Ltd were to buy not less than 75 per cent of his Drapery Trust's shares at 30s. plus a commis sion of 1s. 4d. on each share for Hatry. The acquisition cost up to £2 350 000 and to finance the deal Hatry's Austin Friars Trust in turn agreed to buy for cash £1.6m in blocks of Debenham Ltd's shares.

In turn the capital of the main Debenham Securities was to be greatly increased and reorganized, with Austin Friars Trust buying out big blocks of existing shares and in turn creating millions of new Debenham Securities shares. The whole deal was of bewildering complexity. Within four days, the details were agreed and preparations made to put necessary resolutions before other shareholders.

A short press announcement was made to a startled City but not until 3 December were other shareholders given more facts. The events at this time were to sour the reputation of Debenhams in the City for several years ahead, and even today it is not easy to explain the rush into obvious stock manipulation.

The fusion of the Drapery Trust with Debenhams was headline news. It was called the creation 'of the greatest drapery distribution organization in this country and probably the world'. Yet shareholders, not privy to the directorial agreements, had great difficulty unravelling the complicated scheme. Who is controlling whom they wondered? The City Editor of *The Times* explained that Debenham interests would still predominate, and said the newspaper had been assured that a simpler amalgamation could not be effected 'owing to a variety of circumstances, including incidentally provisions of the company law'.

Ernest Debenham, who had retired from the board of Debenham Securities, according to *The Times* 'had desired to dispose of his shares, and the purchase of his shares was the first transaction'. This remark drew an immediate retort from the retiring chairman in a published letter to The Editor. He wrote:

A month ago I had no intention of retiring from the management of Debenhams. Indeed, I had every reason to hope that the connection of myself and my family with that business would be indefinitely prolonged. When the offer was made to purchase all or any of the Ordinary shares in Debenhams Securities, circumstances of no interest to the general investing public compelled me to accept the offer.

Defending his historic decision to end more than a century of family control of Debenhams, Ernest Debenham said, before going, he had to satisfy himself that control remained with former partners and assured continuity of policy in regard to the staff and that the position of shareholders would not be prejudiced.

Inspection of letters in the archives confirms that Ernest Debenham on 22 November 1927 laid down conditions for the sale of his 1 251 232 shares out of the 2 000 000 controlled by directors of Debenham Securities. They showed on that same day arrangements made for future directorial representation, plus service agreements. However, they also record agreement to complete the purchase of Ernest Debenham's Ordinary shares forthwith, on acceptance (given also on 22 November) of Hatry's terms for merging. He received £1 876 848 for his shares.

In short, control of Debenhams' retailing and warehousing group had now passed from the Debenhams and Olivers (who sold out the previous year) to a pool of directors led by F. H. Richmond, now made chairman of Debenham Securities, and nominees from Hatry's interests. Fortunes were made and secured in a merry-go-round of paper and the inevitable call to the public to subscribe new cash for new shares or switch one piece of security paper for another.

The New Year brought the formal reconstruction of the capital of Debenhams Securities, now controlling Debenhams Ltd and its interests as well as the Drapery Trust. Capital of the master company was increased from £2m in £1 Ordinary shares and £1.5m of £1 Preference shares (total £3.5m) to £4.5m (comprising 3m £1 Preference shares and 6m Ordinary shares of 5 shillings each). Existing holders of Preference shares were given options to sell for cash or convert to the new shares with a small cash payment and proportionate rights to buy the new 5s. Ordinary shares.

Hatry's Austin Friars Trust arranged with M. Samuel & Co. to sell £2m of the new Preference shares to the public and 4 000 000 of the new 5s. Ordinary were allotted to the Trust at par for cash.

In January 1928, Debenhams Securities' subsidiary, Debenhams Ltd acquired 99.8 per cent of the issued Ordinary capital of the Drapery Trust for £2.3m, so clearing up the mystery of who ran the new departmental store empire and ensuring its future.

In the maze of contemporary records and prospectuses, it is all too easy to miss the subtleties of share manipulation by individuals with power over a company's destiny. There are hints of jockeying for position and amalgamating with a competitor in trade which may or may not provide trails for those eager to search out any long-buried skeletons or boardroom rows. What mattered, in the event, was that Debenhams had merged with a huge national group of stores, which had to be organized and run to earn profits. Some 15 000 employees had to be guided and they worked for disparate stores of all shapes and sizes with line management which, by their enthusiasm or lack of it after such a traumatic merger, could make or break the group no longer run by a Debenham and created with the guile and wizardry of a shadowy financier with a doubtful past.

Debenhams had to face up to the stark reality after all the flying paper public share offers, and legal documentation, and to the fact that the new team at the top had to run an empire which ranged from glamorous West End stores to humble popular credit traders in small towns. They rose to the seemingly impossible task of maintaining control over such a rambling collection of enterprises.

Frederick Richmond had worked with Ernest Debenham and Fred Oliver since incorporation and exerted a final authority over what would prove an exercise which sorted out the talent in the higher echelons, whether in the boardroom or outside it. There were many men in management who had independent means (through the sale of their businesses to Hatry's Trust) but whose continued association with family businesses meant they had power to determine the success of Debenhams' performance. Performance there had to be, for 1928 was the year of the Great Slump and widespread social upheaval which in 1929 brought a General Election and the return of a minority Labour Government.

Today, as memories dim, the few people in positions to watch the process of post-merger reorganization speak of certain dominant people whose efforts secured Debenhams against what might have been spectacular disaster. They refer particularly to G. M. Wright, whose brilliance was a match for Hatry in the merger negotiations and whose skills were sorely tried in preserving working capital and funding reorganization. Another was F. J. Pope, a Gloucester family trader whom many Debenhams men now call 'the master trader of C Group', and who brought in big profits in the 1930s but never attained the full directorial majesty he deserved.

But there were serious setbacks before such men could demonstrate their talents.

In 1929 Vesuvius erupted – and so did the City of London as a scandal broke from which Debenhams fortunately emerged unharmed.

A special meeting of the Committee of the Stock Exchange was called on 21 September 1929, amid wild rumours. Hatry and some business associates were being interviewed by the Director of Public Prosecutions following police inquiries into alleged frauds on various loan stock certificates. The Exchange suspended certain dealings and, by October, Hatry stocks and shares were subject to a blockade on settlement dates. Hatry was in custody, refused bail. Among the shares caught up in the whirlwind of the Hatry crash were Preference shares of the Drapery Trust. Dealing in these was stopped, but Ordinary shares had restarted after a shaken Debenhams took full custody of the Trust's share registers and statutory books.

The recently knighted chairman of Debenham Securities, Sir Frederick Richmond, rushed out press statements that securities of the Trust had been verified as free from any irregularity and in good order. Everyone at Debenhams was stunned but relief soon followed that the group had escaped relatively unscathed, though some protracted legal negotiations took place with bankers over Preference shares.

As others crashed or plunged into confusion, the Debenham Securities board whistled amongst themselves at the closeness of what could have been their scandal too. Yet public confidence was shaken in Debenhams, which had so recently negotiated with a man who received twelve years' penal servitude for delivering the greatest blow to City integrity since the South Sea Bubble. The Ordinary shares of Debenham Securities plunged and the chairman and directors, now holding 27 per cent, desperately sought to hold confidence, even offering to buy shares from staff.

The Drapery Trust comprised seventy stores run by thirty-one companies, but few shoppers knew of their ownership by or association with Debenhams. Whatever the ownership, they were all experiencing a fall in profits and poor trading results. The British economy was in dire straits. An important acquisition by Debenhams of the big Pauldens store group of Manchester could not relieve the gloom, even though it brought in new turnover and men.

Britain plunged onwards to an ever deepening financial crisis and the formation of a National Government led by Ramsay Macdonald. Slumping profits and share prices were battering business everywhere. There was little good news. April 1931 brought an action by Lloyds Bank against the Drapery Trust in respect of irregular Preference share transfers, for the ramifications of Hatry's still unravelling deeds were causing problems all round the City and industry.

From the chairman there came in January 1933 a promise that a turning point had arrived. Sir Frederick Richmond wrote in a staff message:

The year that has just closed has been a most difficult and anxious one for all of us. The hopes that we entertained a year ago that 1932 would see the beginnings of a trade revival have, unfortunately, not been fulfilled. The whole world is still under the cloud of economic depression, trade between nations has become more and more restricted, and distress and unemployment are rife in all countries. There is no need for me to dwell on such questions as war debts and disarmament and the various other causes of international misunderstandings which in my view are at the root of all our distresses. The solution of these difficult and highly controversial problems must be left to politicians and economists. So far as our own business is concerned what we have to do is to carry on steadfastly under existing conditions and endeavour to the best of our ability worthily to uphold the traditions of the past.

We may, perhaps, find some encouragement in the thought that, disappointing though the record of the past year has been, it is not unreasonable to assume that we have at long last passed the low water mark of the depression. We are, unfortunately, too close to the subject to see things in their true perspective. Yet, even to-day, bright spots are visible here and there, and although one does not like to be too confident, it may be that when the history of the time comes to be written, the year 1932 will be seen to have been the turning point.

But depressed sales were to remain the main headache in 1933.

As far as Debenhams was concerned, the directors tried to boost morale as best they could while studies were set in hand on how to reverse declining profits. Those at the top encouraged the staff magazine to maintain a continuity of information about the activities that mark the close-knit world of shop staff – rowing, golf, lectures, and news of personal events touching employees of all kinds. Yet Debenhams was plunging towards a crisis.

The man of the moment proved to be G. M. Wright, whose financial recommendations were severe – a comprehensive rewriting of capital and a complete merger of Debenhams, the Drapery Trust and the controlling interests of Debenham Securities. Put starkly, the plan was to reduce the reorganized group's capital. By a series of share revaluations, cancellations and other changes, the combined issued capital was to be spectacularly slashed from £15 100 000 to £6 000 000.

A large unremunerative slab of capital was removed. It was a clever piece of work which, when taken before the High Court in January 1934 for approval, attracted Mr Justice Eve's praise as 'absolutely fair' in the distribution of the impact on shareholders of all classes.

The bit had been taken between the teeth. Such a capital reorganization brought a sense of realism, and a consolidated balance sheet would present a more conservative and considered view of the group's position.

The stern self-discipline now being imposed by Sir Frederick Richmond on investors and shareholding directors had prompted a leading article in the *Financial Times* on 20 December 1933. This stated:

Few even among the least sanguine and most farseeing of industrial leaders can claim fairly to have conceived in advance the full extent of the unprecedented collapse with which home and international trade has been confronted during recent years. Many drastic revisions of capital accounts have testified already to that fact. The latest is as eloquent as any of the penalties of what now are shown to have been exaggeratedly optimistic expansion plans, although at the time they were fashioned and financed they attracted little or no criticism. The severe writing down now to be done by the Debenhams – Drapery Trust group reflects in the luxury trades conditions parallel with those which have already necessitated comparable action in the heavy and other industries. The error of over-expansion and excessive capitalization was committed in large and good company. The process of recognizing and embodying in balance-sheets the facts of today in place of the fancies of yesterday is an unpleasant but unavoidable application of self-discipline.

Staff appeared to view this turmoil with a surprising calm. They had no pension scheme. Two approved employees benefit societies (merged in 1938) dealt with sick benefits, one for manual and one for non-manual staffs. Tailors, cutters and dressmakers making up articles for sale were treated differently from clerical hands, showroom assistants, and salesmen. Benefits were discriminatory up to 1924 and added to state provisions. Yet by 1930 staff were paid reasonably well by the prevailing standards and worked in warm, often pleasant, surroundings. Staff dining rooms served a choice of hot lunches for 10d.

Sport was looked upon with great favour by all London store managements. Each Saturday, duties permitting, teams would take to field, river, or

track. Soccer players would clash with rival teams from Selfridges, or th
Cavendish rowing club (one of the great names of the towpath) woul
match itself against the Harrods eight. There was a pride among cricke
teams, for they were not without their stars, and the greatest was the Mid
dlesex and England Test player G. O. Allen, also of Debenhams
Debenhams helped to make netball history in the summer of 1927 when it
women's team turned out for London against Birmingham in a bid to plac
the game on a national basis, like hockey and lacrosse, under a new Al
England Women's Netball Association. Innumerable trophies change
hands through the twenties and thirties as directors played against staff o
golf greens, or assorted teams of travellers met buyers annually on cricke
pitches. Winners of athletic events frequently graced the picture pages o
staff magazines and bulletins. Managements beamed benevolently on sucl
healthy pursuits.

Theatre was another well supported pastime. Countless people serve
their time in drama groups. Debenhams maintained such a high standar
that productions were frequently mounted in the West End theatres, such a
the Fortune, even attracting national newspaper critics. Sir James Marchant
passionate advocate of 'a cathedral of drama to keep alive the soul of Eng
land', intriguingly chose to argue the case for building a National Theatre i
a special article in Debenhams' humble house journal. Theatre bookin
agencies were operated through many department stores.

There were employees' libraries at Wimpole Street and Harvey Nichol
(five books for a penny a week). Some staff could afford holidays abroad an
a few went for ten days in Nice (£12) or seven days in Paris (£7 12s. 6d.)
with the prices including travel tickets, hotel expenses and excursion
arranged by Pickfords in the Haymarket.

A single sales lady could obtain a furnished bed-sitting room at Lancaste
Gate for 12s. 6d. a week rental. She could, alternatively, go into a Clu
Home, paying in 1928 for example, 25s. weekly for a cubicle 'with sla
partitions and lockable doors'. Full breakfast and use of the lounge went wit
the cubicle. Bathrooms had penny-in-the-slot meters and a three-cours
dinner could be bought for 1s. 6d.

Debenham's main directors may with good humour have presented cup
at staff events, but they had now become remote figures, names in newspap
ers or portraits in the house journal. Perhaps it was appropriate, for th
board had much secret anxiety and they naturally wanted this kept from th
staff. The anxiety concerned both the state of trade and managerial struc
ture.*

*In 1934 Sir Frederick Richmond told shareholders at the annual meeting th
had they in 1927 and 1928 appreciated 'the unprecedented conditions' which wer
going to arise in the next three years it was 'more than probable they would no
have purchased shares of the Drapery Trust, nor sanctioned refixturing and decora
tion of its business.'

Problems quickly arose with Swan & Edgar, caught up in the Hatry deals. The giant of Regent Street and Piccadilly had been Queen Victoria's favourite store, and William Edgar used to ride to town from his Kingston Hill home, on his horse Enfield, a proud and handsome figure. Harrods had assumed control for a period and began construction of a new store, held up by the Great War as well as by squabbles among architects concerned to preserve the grand sweep of the frontages. The new premises were opened in June 1927, not long after the Drapery Trust gained a shareholding.

After the Trust's subsequent deal with Debenhams, the latter's holding in Swan & Edgar was still less than 50 per cent. The ruling Scase family had a majority of boardroom votes against Debenham nominees and throughout the thirties successfully resisted periodic challenge to change its policies. Swan & Edgar men wanted to be left alone to run the giant store in their style. They got their way.

After the capital reorganization, Debenham's directors, now numbering fifteen, followed a conservative policy in regard to the distribution of dividends, and £59 000 was set aside every year in order to build up a reserve. For the next three years the profits rose steadily, reaching a figure of £728 000 in 1937. The number of trading units in the country was then seventy-seven, of which four were wholesale. Up to the outbreak of the Second World War, four retail businesses were acquired, namely Pauldens, Manchester (1930), Arnolds, Great Yarmouth (1936), J. K. Hubbard, Worthing (1937) and Lefevres, Gillingham (1939).

The timing of a massive capital reorganization had been well chosen, for retail trade began slowly to pick up and, with its wide spread of stores, Debenhams felt the benefits while servicing less capital. There was a new optimism in the air and middle management morale, always quick to react to trouble, picked up rapidly.

Few could know that these years of reviving consumer confidence would be cut short by the end of the decade. Britain seemed too preoccupied with her own social upheaval and economic recovery to notice that across the North Sea in 1933 Hitler had been appointed Chancellor of Germany by Hindenberg, who died the following year. More alert world statesmen then blanched as the Fuehrer became dictator of a new Reich.

6 Bargain basements and elephants

Miss Dorothy Marno's Bohemian Orchestra trying out the new organ in Kennards restaurant after the final tuning. This organ, the first to be built in the restaurant of any store in London, will be officially opened by Mr Haydn Wood, the popular composer, this Saturday October 7, 1935, at 3.30 p.m.

Caption to photograph in the *Croydon Advertiser*.

Refreshing winds blew across the British economy from 1933, reviving the tired and panting retail trade. Up to 23 per cent of the insured population had been unemployed and the years of the gold standard had given way to international monetary crisis, and Britain seemed in decline between 1929 and 1932. Businesses failed as Governments managed the currency and began to intervene in industry. A marked revival in world trade by the mid-thirties, however, came none too soon to an ailing economy, and there was to be expansion in new industries, such as motor vehicles and electrical goods. Employment in distribution, a barometer for the business climate, increased sharply as real incomes began to rise.

Basic industries did not, however, surge with a new vigour. The textiles industries were being paralysed by overseas competition, particularly cotton, and order books remained thin. Yet there were significant pointers to the future. Rayon production rose sharply, doubling between 1929 and 1937. New consumer goods such as refrigerators and canned foods began to appear. Radio and later television sets began to sell in great quantity. Housebuilders threw up thousands of cheap homes around big cities, particularly London which was now well served by underground and regular train services. A new *Road Traffic Act* signalled the importance of the motor car in national life.

Retailers noted one intriguing element in recovery. This was the substitution of *homo econonomicus* by a new species, economic woman, who began to emerge as the main administrator in the thirties household, managing family budgets for the first time. Women thought very differently. They were subject to impulse but shopping was a dimension in their lives not always fully appreciated by mere males, who thought it drudgery and a question of providing a limited sum of housekeeping money each week. Women had latent skills in judging relative values and, after years of 'making do and

George VI's coronation procession passing Swan & Edgar

*Marshall & Snelgrove
centenary catalogue
Above: Formal day dress
with soutache braiding
Top left: Camel hair
travelling coats
Top right: Model hat in
Bantall straw
Below left: Lace court dress
Below right: Evening gown
and coatee with applique
chiffon flowers*

mend', were not just concerned with material judgements in making purchases. New fashions and great variety in selling clothes and other essentials coincided with the arrival of new products. Consumers had choice, and women became a dominant influence in deciding not only what to buy but where to make their purchases.

National life brightened and radio brought cohesion. American cinema movies, presented in grand new picture palaces, continued to build up expectations of a higher standard of living. Fierce circulation battles between newspapers showed that the pennies of the masses counted. Newspapers offered space to a new breed of advertisers attempting to reach women and, to ensure the necessary readership, promoted special pages of fashion and news orientated towards feminine interests. A great variety of popular magazines were launched or re-styled. Drapers and store operators of all kinds observed the impact on dress and life styles.

Not even the death at 70 of George V or the Abdication Crisis of Edward VIII in 1936 could shake the revival of confidence. As a Prime Minister, Stanley Baldwin was confident and reassuring. The twenties had had their gaiety, but only for some, and now the lower middle classes and working people wanted their fun. Day trips to the seaside and even holidays away from home, if without pay, became possible for many ordinary families. For its part, Debenhams was faced with new spending patterns and more goods to stock. A management bred in the London emporia to deal with the carriage trade had to come to terms with the fact that the more popular stores it had inherited proved to be a source of great profits. Stores were grouped according to classification of trade, popular to medium class, high class, and just popular.

The Coronation in 1937 of George VI unleashed a wave of celebratory spending and commercial exploitation of the event. Every home in the land bought souvenirs and stores showed great ingenuity in supplying everything from flags and commemorative tea sets to toys and tea towels. The year was a rather special one, too, for the great Marshall & Snelgrove celebrated its centenary. There were lavish ceremonies and great floral displays greeted customers. The latest in lifts was commissioned to mark the occasion.

Marshall & Snelgrove did not make much money, in spite of its reputation and the obvious excellence of its service. Ownership, however, brought great goodwill to Debenhams, whose directors appeared to regard its standards with a constant admiration that belied its importance to earnings compared with the popular provincial stores. There was no doubt that Marshall & Snelgrove was one of the world's most famous stores.

Founded in 1837 by a 31-year-old Yorkshireman James Marshall at 11 Vere Street, London, the business began under the name Marshall & Wilson, later Marshall, Wilson & Stinton. But within eleven years Marshall had met John Snelgrove, son of a Somerset paper manufacturer who claimed he came to London on foot with just half a crown and a wish to learn retailing. The founder's eldest son, James C. Marshall, turned the enterprise into a national institution by acquiring an Oxford Street frontage in 1851 and raising a new building, the Royal British Warehouse, for the Victorian carriage trade.

The Marshall family was far sighted, pioneering half-day closing, and its

E. J. Marshall

wealth was expressed by the founder's 1000-acre estate, Goldbeaters, at Mi[ll]
Hill, North London, with a 1¼-mile carriage drive. His youngest son was [a]
popular hero, an All England cricketer, while the eldest concentrated o[n]
business. One of James C. Marshall's most important decisions was to ope[n]
great stores in Scarborough and Harrogate, followed by others in Birming[-]
ham, Manchester, Southport, Leicester, Leeds, York, Sheffield, and Brad[-]
ford. He died in 1925 aged 95, by which time the firm had been merged wit[h]
Debenhams. To this day, loyal ex-employees live in sheltered cottage home[s]
on land at Mill Hill donated by James Marshall, who was keen on draper[y]
charities.

Things happened in and around Marshall & Snelgrove. Some were reca[l-]
led years later in 1926 by a book reviewer in the *Manchester Guardian* writin[g]
about the life of Henry Chaplin. Chaplin had 'made manful ducks and drake[s]
with a fortune and a great estate', and, in 1864, something he did cause[d]

ridicule in London society. No one is sure exactly what happened, but it certainly took place at Marshall & Snelgrove's in Oxford Street. In its version, the *Manchester Guardian* records:

It is curious that this establishment, still flourishing and famous among us, should have entwined itself not once but two or three times in the most eminent worthies of the Conservative party. At another time Mr and Mrs Gladstone were conspicuously touched by the beauty of a birthday message sent to them by the assistants at Marshall & Snelgrove's. And then there was this story about the young Henry Chaplin and the very high-born beauty who was to have been his bride – how only a few hours before the wedding day he drove her in a dog-cart to the shop; how she went in at the front door and out at the back; how she met the Marquis of Hastings a famous roué of the times; and how while Mr Chaplin was waiting for her in the one street she was at the church in the other, becoming the Marquis of Hastings' wife. So it used to be said!

The thirties were vital, lusty years for Debenhams. With its plethora of stores ranging from the southern Bobbys to the great names of Scottish store-keeping, its managers and staff had room to expand and to try out new ideas. Their individual initiatives were designed to produce trading results demonstrating that department stores could survive against competition from newer chain stores, entrenched cooperative societies, new multiples, and a host of little men hoping to grow – for the dream of many couples was still to own a small shop and to join the merchant classes. Within Debenhams, there were many executives who bore the names of founding families associated with the stores now controlled by the organization and they were a new generation with decided ideas about how to adapt department stores to popular demands. Their admiration for the ideas of F. J. Pope flowed from the astonishing gains he had made in running Bon Marché in Gloucester and from his eagerness to influence other stores. Pope emerged as the significant figure in popular trading.

In sharp contrast to the energetic Pope, who trained several generations of Debenham executives, was G. Maurice Wright. The Hatry affair had left its mark on Wright's attitude towards the City, and for years he resisted suggestions for widening Debenhams' contacts beyond those known to Sir Frederick Richmond and himself. Yet his influence on financial policy was beyond challenge. The sheer complexities of Debenhams at this time were apparently understood only by Wright, who was insular by instinct but often full of bonhomie towards those who recognized his internal authority.

Wright was to reform accounting systems, often staging large secretariat conferences to impress on everyone the need for more unity among stores in keeping their books. While Pope was driving salesmen, Wright poured over bought ledgers and reformed counting houses, though sometimes with reluctance when it came to hard spending decisions (there was an internal fight over new mechanized systems for recording transactions which initially would cost more to run but promised great economies after some years of operation).

Oval-faced and always well dressed, Wright was rich from his early association with Ernest Debenham. He smoked big cigars continuously and

Fred Pope

sported an expensive time-piece strung on a chain across fashionable waist-coats. The hair was always slick and neatly parted. He looked ambitious, bu prudence had replaced ambition. Reforms flowed from caution, bred by the trauma of capital reorganizations in times of slump. He was content to le Pope bring in more profits.

Fred Pope was the driving force of the provincial stores. He had been trained in the family business of Bon Marché in Gloucester, which had a big reputation for aggressive trading. Pope was inherited with the Drapery Trust, and given the task of organizing what became known as C Group, the rather military internal code name for medium to popular stores, distin-guishing them from the big London stores and a few others grouped respec-tively into A and B classifications.

Pope understood bulk buying, especially the fashion requirements o women, and visited stores regularly to encourage managers and sales staff He could be found on Saturday afternoons, even when given heavy respon-sibilities in London, packing up coats in the women's department of some store, keeping in touch with customers and always checking stock policies His visits and regular talks with groups of managers were not always popu-lar, but gradually his authority was established.

This was no mean feat. The fact was that Debenhams was a federation o highly individual stores, or groups of shops, run by people often drawn from their founding families. A managing director of one of these businesses would cherish his autonomy and position whenever threatened by outside interference. Ownership by the Debenhams group did not mean automatic deference to the central management. Pope won over store chiefs, one by one, and many a meeting at his estate near Cheltenham helped obtain increas-ing cooperation in reform of stock and promotion policy. The biggest prob-lem was the buyers in the largest stores. Pope's policy, when confronted with stock that proved slow to sell, was to clear it at bargain prices and to encourage stores to build up sufficient reserves to cover any losses. But there were plenty of buyers unwilling to admit to mistakes in their ordering hanging onto goods and over-valuing them in their books in a forlorn hope of eventual sales.

With his star in the ascendant, Pope the hard trader was, however, to prove somewhat unpopular around Debenhams' headquarters. His success compared with the London prestige stores in turning in big profits, was changing the power structure, and he was to be kept off a key central management committee where his ideas might have made a more radical impact on future policy.

---

*In the mid-thirties, Debenhams placed all provincial stores (excepting the Bobby, Plummer and Marshall stores, the big London stores, and the Scottish Drapery Corporation) under the control of F. J. Pope. The Pope stores were then known as the 'C' Group. In 1939, 'C' Group comprised: Bon Marché of Gloucester Spooners of Plymouth, Edwin Jones of Southampton, William Lefevre of Canter-bury, Lefevres of Gillingham, Footman Pretty of Ipswich, Curls of Norwich, Jones of Bristol, Pauldens of Manchester, Arnolds of Great Yarmouth, and Smiths o Nuneaton, Stratford, and Bedworth.

There were two schools of managers – those reared in the grand traditions of West End trading and those who saw higher earnings from coordinating and concentrating talent on the stores outside London. New men, such as the aggressive Arthur Bobby, whose stores ranged from medium to better, and who was keen on pricing against competitors, were to become Pope men. Other supporters could be found in Bristol and Southampton and they were actively to assist Pope when he began experimenting with the concept of buying goods in bulk and marketing these in departments around the country.

Many of Pope's ideas were viewed with suspicion by more than a few buyers employed within semi-autonomous stores. They naturally saw their role and status being eroded if the scheme took root. Yet there were more than a few individual stores which just could not afford to employ expert buyers, and lost those they had through retirements. Other stores were just missing sales because the buyers lacked expertise in buying new products which they had not previously handled. From Pope, however, came the first modest efforts at coordinated buying between stores. Welbeck Fashion Service was created, and Debenhams Limited Manufacturing and Supplies was established to develop a rudimentary form of central buying.

Brought in to run DLMS, as it became the habit of Debenhams men to call it, was Imrie Swainston, a flamboyant character whose manner did not always endear him to conservative buyers. Small stores, however, were quick to appreciate DLMS offers. Swainston, who was to leave Debenhams and set up a rival operation called Textile and General Suppliers, showed that there was a demand for the well planned central marketing of goods. He demonstrated this with heavy sales of Vereston double sheets at 9s. 11d. per pair and Golden Dawn ladies 'locknit' underwear sets at 4s. 11d. each.

Window display of Vereston fabrics at Jones of Bristol

The limited exercises in coordinated buying caused great internal argu
ment, which was inevitable given that Debenhams was the sum of man
talented individuals with different styles and backgrounds. Like all larg
enterprises, and it was common to Government and Whitehall, the conflic
had to be reduced by forming committees. These were set up and comprise
men handpicked from the various stores, known for their ability to persuad
others to a common point of view.

These committees undertook the task of preparing bulk orders an
specifications from suppliers of such items as coats and blouses. Then the
were offered to the stores. It was a clumsy system, yet there were man
successes. Some 40 000 camel wool coats, for example, were pushed quickl
through the stores at 29s. 11d. each. In spite of such obvious demonstration
of public response to the well executed marketing operation, there was n
obligation on individual Debenham stores to take instructions from th
centre, and individual managing directors were constantly listening to th
complaints of their local buyers who would be ignored. The consequence
were to be felt years later, though it is a matter of speculation as to whethe
central buying would have been delayed unduly. The Second World Wa
ended arguments.

The ideas of Pope and his 'C' men were regarded with some apprehensio
at the top of Debenhams. Sir Frederick Richmond, by now a gentlema
farmer and moving in remote social circles out of sight to those below him
operated from luxurious offices on the fourth floor of a building in Wimpo
Street. Pope liked to get away from this atmosphere whenever he could
disliking the constant preoccupation of the board with the London stores
which always featured strongly in annual reports contrary to the hard facts c
where profits were made. Yet Richmond was not a foolish figure. On th
contrary, he was greatly concerned that the wholesale activities c
Debenhams, beginning to find life more difficult, should not be damaged b
aggressive retailing which undermined the wholesale company's customers
Competitors who bought goods from Debenhams the wholesaler did nc
view Pope's aggressiveness too kindly, and demanded equal treatment o
terms, believing Debenhams was subsidizing its own marketing at thei
expense.

Nonetheless, there is no doubt that Richmond also disapproved of th
brasher men always talking about popular shopkeeping, using their depart
ment stores to stage ever bolder sales events to attract customers and t
promote their name as price cutters in local communities. Bargain base
ments, as many lower floors became, could make the chairman visibly shud
der. Yet he could not deny the reality of the figures when they came in frot
Wright's office.

Popular shopping was all very well, but it seemed standards might sli
Stores which splashed whitewash messages across their windows an
replaced carpets with lino and low-cost fittings were evidently not trying t
copy the big London stores. In between were the comfortable quality store
of county towns and provincial cities, unsure whether changes to attra
wider custom might harm their traditions of service and that certain atmos
phere of exclusivity which they carefully preserved. Shopfitters found popu

Above: *Interior of a C shop*

Below: *Jimmy Driscoll*

lar stores ready to innovate. Many people today have childhood memories of Emmett-like contraptions for carrying cash and invoices across ceilings and down walls. There were clanking continuous belts, mechanisms for catapulting screw canisters over customers' heads, and pneumatic tubes. Wall to ceiling drawers would be slid in and out, and glass cases replaced wooden counters.

Debenhams' men still talk about one particular store chief, Jimmy Driscoll, who ran Kennards of Croydon with the flair of a theatrical impressario. Driscoll was a brilliant window dresser, and his displays were constantly changed, eschewing the conservative methods of West End dressers. Driscoll, in the thirties, was reprimanded by the chairman after he appeared in court for obstructing the North End in the central shopping area of Croydon. He had been 'carted' off to the police station when two elephants, loaned by Bertram Mills Circus to promote a 'Jumbo' birthday sales event, brought the town centre to a halt. Pauldens of Manchester and Bobbys in the South pioneered the use of personalities to open sales events and stores, enlisting everyone from Amy Johnson, the aviator, to Henry Hall's leading singer Betty Driver (better known these days for her role in the TV saga *Coronation Street*). Store managers hand-delivered brochures and notices around new housing estates. Their premises were used for exhibitions, to build up flows of people. Local organizations were given facilities to hold meetings, and those with restaurants began to compete hard for catering contracts, large and small.

117

Popularized stores varied, but the emphasis was on ready cash sales. The trade of professional people was valued, but they tended to expect credit and personal accounts which they were slow to settle. Doctors were noted as some of the slowest.

Many stores had tea rooms and restaurants where trios played music and requests. Smiths of Stratford-on-Avon initiated 'Buyers Events' in 1934 using advertisements carrying photographs of their buyers over lists of their bargain offers. The flagship of the big Bobby group, although started in Margate, was its Bournemouth store, which sold aggressively to the holiday trade. Musical acts appeared at coffee mornings and teatime. In the evening there was always a cabaret act. Events at Bournemouth of all kinds ranged from displaying the world's largest opal to practical beauty demonstrations and fashion shows.

Each store or grouping had its own ideas. One exclusive Exeter store never gave farthings in change, only packets of pins, and the pins 'sold' added up to a considerable sum. Plummers of Hastings engaged 'Koringa and her Crocodile', described as a Female Fakir, to bring in the crowds and an endless succcession of celebrities entertained in the restaurant.

Yet there was no one to match the enterprising Driscoll, who arrived in England from Australia and had worked at Whiteleys and Barkers before joining Kennards of Croydon. He introduced 'Clock Days', when bargains were offered as each hour struck. There were managing director's blue pencil days when he would march at the head of a column of shoppers with a blue pencil, slashing prices along the way. He printed cartoons in newspapers depicting his buyers groaning at some foolhardy event to take place shortly. A new cash-and-carry store was opened in 1932, promising quick service and nothing over five shillings.

Driscoll was the retail trade's great showman of the thirties. A Wurlitzer organ was installed in the Kennards restaurant and there was always some free show ranging from display of Sir Malcolm Campbell's world land speed record breaking car Blue Bird to some sportsman of the day giving out tips. There was a resident band, Dorothy Marno's Bohemian orchestra. Film stars, guards bands, even Dukes, joined the fun. He offered merchandise worth 28 shillings for gold sovereigns, scrolls giving customers freedom of the store, donkey rides, and tours of the main cash desk where pneumatic tubes blew in money from 150 sales stations around the store. There were dog weeks, and a pet corner with a children's club.

He staged a Wild West 'Shoot Out' between Two-Gun Rix and Ranger Cliff Norman, featuring 'an amazing display of shooting, roping, knife throwing and mulish viciousness'. He pioneered Christmas toy fairs, now so commonplace, and small shops within his store.

In spite of reprimand for the elephant incident, Driscoll was unrepentant. He was even allowed by Debenhams to buy his own store at Wimbledon but to use the Kennards name. Ideas were thought up while driving around in his 1936 two-seater supercharged 'Auborn' car. He was to make the men at Debenham & Freebody, Marshall & Snelgrove and Harvey Nichols shudder as the latest stories of his exploits circulated. Fred Pope, who encouraged Driscoll, just watched the sales and profits.

Driscoll was one of the early showmen. Cinema managers would adapt his ideas of staging promotional events to make people come to their premises, even just to call in to be reminded that patrons counted. Another was William Paulden, who in Manchester in the late nineteenth century bought one of the first electric lifts and had window displays featuring live lions and tigers. Pauldens was later a major promoter of brass band competitions.

One display manager with forty-two years' experience, Mr H. B. Fisher, now retired, recalls an Easter Farm staged on the open roof of Pauldens. Flocks of sheep, goats, cows and other farmyard animals were taken through the store onto the roof. Unfortunately, there was to be a late snowfall which blocked the roof entrance. The animals had to be rescued by ladders and ropes from outside the building.

The popular stores were in another world for Sir Frederick, whose heart was very much in the Debenham & Freebody which he had personally controlled, even if his head told him of the necessity of 'C' division. Gross trading margins ranged from 20 per cent for Smiths in the Midlands to 24 per cent at Bon Marché, Gloucester, and 33 per cent at Bobby's stores.

In London mark-ups were high and overheads soared. The maintenance of lavish facilities in prestigious stores was important to their particular sales image. Lots of upholstered seats and settees, chandeliers, cloakrooms with full carpeting and well appointed rest rooms were refuges for those who wished to purchase their requirements in style and comfort. Behind the scenes there were teams of seamstresses and bespoke tailors.

In far away Southampton, the Jones store entered the food business and installed a team of girls with telephone head-sets to take customers' orders for delivery by a fleet of electric vehicles.

The new food hall at Edwin Jones

Sir Frederick Richmond presenting cheques to long-serving employees

Away from the bustle of the 'C' group stores, Sir Frederick Richmond retained his deep affection for the great London houses he knew so well. He was not inconsiderate, just attached to the past, which was his yardstick for excellence. Some very grand offices were provided for those around him but his own, in 1937, was not extravagant by some standards. There was a small, rather plain desk, at which he sat, often sporting a spotted bow tie as a personal relief from the severity of his suits and 'knife-cut' hair parting. He disliked clutter, and would toy with a special ink blotter, while some manager sat stiffly in front of him, trying not to notice the rather incongruous *art nouveau* picture hanging on the wall behind the chairman. Periodically, Richmond would hand over cheques to long-serving employees ushered into his room for a short talk on their retirement. Men still working at 70 or more were not uncommon, and a ceremony for 50 years' service was not infrequent.

Richmond did much for the London he loved, particularly the Wigmore and Welbeck Streets area. He led the endowment of a ward at the Middlesex Hospital, where he was a governor and served on various charitable institutions. The Cottage Homes thrived with his support. Yet the chairman was an elevated figure to everyone, proud of his directorship of the historic Hudson's Bay Company and his acquaintance with influential people of the kind who expected genuflecting service in some West End stores, which in truth only just paid their way.

The remoteness of the chairman is recalled by Jack Smith, who rose from a family business to Debenhams' main board. He recalled 'Whenever I saw Richmond, the chairman would say, "Ah, Smith isn't it – you are the

Nuneaton fellow with the store with a river running through it." ' This identification of people with premises indicated the divided times.

From the late twenties, women had been employed in great numbers. Jobs in department stores were coveted and women bought their own sales dresses, which they kept in lockers. Some rose through the ranks to become buyers, but men still strictly controlled the big fashion decisions. Jack Mullins, who worked under Pope, said it was generally held that women tended to look at merchandise from the point of view of suitability for their personal use. Men bought goods because they felt they would look well on women at large and were harsher judges of what was a fine design and what was a design which would sell in great quantities. Clothing fashions drew their inspiration from Paris, London and New York, but popular stores always waited to catch the tide of a changing style. Always be second in fashion, whilst the first burnt their fingers, was Pope's advice for his class of trade. But he was harsh if the style was missed, and the new chain stores stole a march on some trend.

In their way, provincial departmental stores were fashion setters in many towns and cities. Many wives in higher income circles were cautious in their purchases, but always reassured if the local department store came up with a style adapted or derived from London fashion circles. Provincial society had a craving for smartness and modernity, but country reserve entered into a store buyer's judgement in satisfying the craving.

Those who lived through the slump and recovery of the thirties were to be divided between those concerned by events in Germany and those preoccupied with Britain's re-emerging economic performance. Nostalgia tends to soften reality. One person deeply troubled in 1934 by the rise of Hitler was Fred Oliver, by now a partial invalid from tuberculosis, and writing against time at his Jedburgh home to complete the third volume of his monumental work, *The Endless Adventure*, for the Macmillan publishing house. He died in June of that year, the summer which brought the death of Hindenburg. In his writings, he had often reflected on German militarism and had caused controversy with his advocacy of military conscription in Britain. His sense of history was rare.

Oliver's own story as the managing director of Debenhams who combined business, literature, and political philosophy had been made all the more remarkable by his constant struggle against consumption.

As a student of Burke and Alexander Hamilton, his mind was perpetually occupied with the question of the development of the British Empire. He had flung himself ardently into Mr Joseph Chamberlain's tariff reform campaign in 1903, and some of his pamphlets, such as his 'Letters of John Draper', addressed to the Bishop of Hereford, were among the best controversial literature of that period. In 1906 he published his *Life of Alexander Hamilton*. The book had probably more influence than any other political work of the decade. It became a textbook for all those up and down the Empire who were giving their minds to Imperial reconstruction. It had a very special and direct influence on the group which conceived and carried through the Union of South Africa. In America, also, its influence was great, and described as devout Jeffersonian in tone.

121

The publication of the book was followed by a period of bad health, but after his recovery Oliver appeared again in current controversy. His friendship with Sir Horace Plunkett gave him an eager interest in the Irish question, and when it became plain that Mr Asquith's Government proposed a scheme of Home Rule, to which Ulster was vigorously opposed, Oliver's was one of the most powerful voices raised in protest. For long he believed that a federal scheme would solve the problem, and he expounded his view under the pseudonym of 'Pacificus' in several striking letters to *The Times* which were afterwards published in pamphlet form. In the spring of 1914 however, he lost hope in the solution, and came to the conclusion that Federalism must wait, since the obligations of Mr Asquith's Government to the Irish Party made it impossible at the moment.

Oliver was also a close student of military matters, and formed one of a group, mostly composed of distinguished soldiers, who supported Lord Roberts in his scheme for national service. When the Great War broke out it seemed to the members of the group that their warnings were more than justified.

In the early summer of 1915 Oliver published a second book, *Ordeal by Battle* which endeavoured to put before the country the meaning of a war of nations. His thesis was that under conditions of modern warfare it is not only armies which need to be disciplined, but whole nations, and he dealt trenchantly with his old *bête noire* – the lawyer-politician.

He asked that the people should be trusted and told the truth, and in a year's time his views were accepted as truisms. The book was described by *The Times* as 'a store-house of political thought, set out with a precision and an eloquence which has long since been absent from the literature of politics'. In many ways, it was the most remarkable English publication of the war.

After the Armistice Oliver's health compelled him to spend much of the year away from London. Early in his career he had bought and later extended a little manor house at Checkendon, in the Chiltern Hills. In 1916 he acquired the estate of Edgerston, at the head of the Jed valley, running up to the watershed of the Cheviots. Here, in the countryside from which his forebears came, he spent most of his time, engaged in the pursuits of a Border laird, but also assiduously working at a history of the eighteenth and early nineteenth centuries, which was intended to show the origins of contemporary movements and institutions in Britain. He wrote and rewrote and his extreme conscientiousness made the work progress slowly.

Ultimately he narrowed his purpose to a study of the career of Sir Robert Walpole, whom he regarded as the typical English politician. The work was entitled *The Endless Adventure*; the first part appeared in 1930, the second in the following year, and he died completing the third part. A most acute and laborious student of history had gone, said *The Times*, in its long obituary.

Oliver's mind had two sides – one strictly logical, delighting in close and compact argument, and the other imaginative and intuitive. He was not one who over-valued procrastination, for he held that in the greater matters of life the mind must 'fling itself forward' and that the possession of this instinct is what constitutes the difference between the great and the less great of mankind. This power he believed to be found chiefly in simple souls, and that explained his admiration for soldiers.

The wise fool seemed to him the worst of all fools. He believed that the ordinary man was the best judge of most things, and might, if lawyers and pedants could be got out of the way, be trusted to govern the country. The worst vice in modern life was seeing the trees and missing the wood, but it was a vice of clever, not of plain, people.

Much can be said for Oliver's judgement that the emergence of Hitler required powerful statesmanship and mobilization of Britain. Within a few years of Oliver's death, Chamberlain went to Munich and many lesser thinkers were suborned into a belief that peace might be secured on the paper promises of a militarist dictator whose adaptation of Oliverian concepts of Empire building flowed more from a lust for power than service. Back in the Parliamentary wilderness was Winston Churchill, a man of action of the kind Oliver so openly admired and wrote about. Churchill had a sense of political destiny and service to an Imperial ideal capable of firing the imagination of ordinary Britons. Oliver's dying interest in Churchill's warnings about Hitler's National Socialism faded from public consciousness amid the events culminating in the Second World War.

Britain declared war on Germany on 3 September 1939. The next day, a liner, the *Athenia*, was torpedoed 250 miles off the Irish coast, yet Britain responded to Hitler by dropping leaflets across Germany. Department stores and all shopkeepers ordered vast quantities of dark materials to black out their windows in case of air-raid attacks and they began checking fire precautions. At first, shoppers would avoid central areas. Theatres and cinemas were shut and football matches postponed, all on Government orders. Shoppers began to carry masks against possible gas attacks on the civilian population, and they cleared stores of such things as torches, candles, canned goods and other items likely to become scarce.

War brought the suspension of many reforms within Debenhams which might have been pressed by directors such as Arthur Bobby and E. W. Strange. For these two men had only a year before its declaration undertaken an intensive tour of the United States, visiting all the big city stores, including J. T. Hudson in Detroit. Yet, even as they travelled, the then managing director, L. Snowden, was personally setting up, within the West End businesses, an auxiliary fire brigade from volunteers from the male staff aged 30 and over 'to deal with outbreaks of fire which might occur in the event of attack by hostile aircraft during the daytime'.

There can be no doubt that Debenhams had foresight about the threat from Germany. It was under no illusion. This is not an idle claim. On 30 March 1937, over 500 men employed by what were called the 'associated houses of Debenhams Ltd' gathered at Wigmore Hall, London, to hear a dissertation from Major General R. H. D. Thompson, on air defence. James Spence, deputy chairman, acted as chairman, flanked by directors and managers.

General Thompson, who commanded the 1st Anti-Aircraft Division, Territorial Army, outlined the work to be done in wartime by the force under his command and stressed the fact that volunteers were needed to bring it up to strength. Although he was sure that, on the outbreak of war, there would be thousands of volunteers, these would be useless as they had not received the necessary specialized training. He said:

If London goes, England goes. If the enemy bomber came over London in day light, and it is hardly to be hoped that he would be so rash, the RAF would deal with him. The fighting planes are so much faster and easier to manoeuvre that they could easily deal with any bomber if they could see him. But what would happen if he came in the dark?

Your fighter planes would be unable to go to the attack. The bomber would choose his ideal height and position to destroy Fulham Power Station, Clapham Junction, the Great North Road, or any of these targets with a certain amount of equanimity. Fortunately, we shall shortly have all the equipment we require to deal with these bombers. Every single site in the vast lay-out which protects the capital is connected by telephone, but the men are not there.

He added that, with the necessary number of men, the searchlight equipment could keep the bomber in the blinding rays of three intersecting beams while the fighter planes could destroy him at will from the angle of their choice. 'But,' continued the General, 'there are a large number of black spots – dark patches where, for want of detachments to work the projectors, we cannot light up the bomber. That is a disaster. What we want at the present moment are additional men who will undertake this job of home defence which cannot be learned in five minutes when war comes.'

Inspection of Debenhams special constables, 1938

There were to be many volunteers from Debenhams to join the Territorial Army. They were encouraged too by Mr Spence's announcement at the end of the meeting that one week's holiday with pay would be given to every member of the staff in the territorials who attended annual camps.

Just before the outbreak of war, the managing director of Pauldens in Manchester was Percy Besley, who became group captain in a Balloon Command. Such was Besley's enthusiasm that he persuaded many buyers and managers into enrolment as auxiliaries. The result was that these people were quickly called up when war was declared, denuding the store of much of its management.

Such was the initial atmosphere of common danger that few could pause to reflect on the death, as war broke out, in far away Australia of one of the few remaining members of the original Debenham family. Robert Debenham had gone to Australia around 1890 to develop a local business and had been succeeded by one of his sons, Arthur. Nonetheless Robert's death rekindled a few London memories, for his eldest son, Keith Debenham, had been killed on active service against Germany in the First World War.

The feeling of shared danger began to ease when bombs did not rain down, nor did gas drift down High Streets. Then came the period now called the 'Phoney War'. Some restrictions on national life were even eased, causing a mood of false optimism. Nonetheless, householders began to register with food shops while the Government dithered over the necessity for introducing food rationing.

What was to be total war began with an *Emergency Powers Act* and confusion among retailers. Dunkirk did not come until May and June 1940, when a new Coalition Cabinet under a national government led by the defiant Churchill took charge. On 5 June 1940, Hitler proclaimed 'a war of total annihilation' against his enemies, and within months Britain was penetrated by enemy aircraft and threatened with possible invasion across her beaches.

War brought the inevitable and rigid central planning required to sustain 45 000 000 people contained within an island whose vital shipping was now imperilled. Emergency legislation and successions of budgets were only part of the bureaucracy built up between 1939 and 1945. Warfare was unremitting in its consumption of capital and people as well as materials. The aim was to limit consumption and choice without disrupting morale on the home front. Once again for the mass of the population it was a time for making do, and no income groups escaped the rigours of regulations and shortages.

The Second World War shattered a great and once rich nation, but it brought the British people together in an unparalleled way to share common adversity. Even today there is great nostalgia, because despite really dreadful privations and losses of life and property, people frequently helped each other. The comradeship of air raid shelters, common danger, queues, and the opening of country homes to evacuees is apt to be recalled by those who lived through it all. Yet this was a time of worsening shortages, arguments about priorities, the emergence of 'black markets', and frequently strained relationships between customers and staff in shops.

The story of war finance, taxation, and the regulation of civil affairs had its prologue in the emergency budget of September 1939. Income tax was set at

125

a standard rate of 7s. 6d. The most momentous change for retailers was the imposition of an excess profits tax of 60 per cent on profits earned above a standard level, plus a national defence contribution from companies.

Two budgets in April and July 1940 raised income tax by stages to 8s. 6d., and to 10s. a year later and increased excess profits tax to 100 per cent. There were also specific decisions of great importance to retailing. For the outbreak of war was to be followed the next summer by the imposition of a purchase tax, introduced at a flat rate but later revised to discriminate against goods classed as luxury or semi-luxury items.

Comparatively early in the war, a Central Price Regulation Committee was set up. This spawned local committees. Their task was to take the profit out of war, what with expected shortages and the imperative needs of the military machine. Big contracts had to be placed for non-civilian goods, including clothing, foodstuffs and all the items needed by expanded armed services and the supporting civilian services, which had been reorganized to make armaments and to act under directions from Whitehall's war administrators.

Bobbys on fire

Few businesses of any size escaped from requisitioning of their premises by various authorities. Enemy bombs did not discriminate. Debenhams had a wide network of stores, many vulnerable to invasion or bombardment along the Eastern and Southern coasts, and others certain targets for any blitz, fire bombing and blasting of major industrial towns or big conurbations. The board had prepared for war early in 1939. The staff journal, *Mayfair One*, ceased publication. Among the precautions were the construction of many air raid shelters within stores to protect staff and customers. Where basements existed, these were re-walled and reinforced with steel supports. In these basement shelters were stored first aid equipment, emergency food supplies, drums of water, chemical closets, axes, torches, and accumulators to feed emergency lighting.

The first store to suffer damage was Bobbys' premises at Torquay, but this was not due to enemy action. A major fire destroyed much of its trading area and makeshift arrangements had to be made for the rest of the war. Another false alarm was at Lefevres in Gillingham – a bus ploughed through the frontage, which then had to be totally bricked up with just two feet of 'peeping window'. Teams of aircraft spotters were trained within Debenhams and, operating by rota, managers and staff daily scanned the skies. Squads of fire watchers were formed, too, practising with buckets and stirrup pumps and running test alarms. Many stores were saved as a result of action taken by these squads, who dealt bravely with incendiary bombs. But sometimes they had to watch helplessly as fire brigades fought to save their stores.

Debenhams took its share of destruction in the High Streets of Britain. Completely destroyed by enemy action were:

1940 Edwin Jones, Southampton; Plummer Roddis, Southampton; Jones, Bristol
1941 Handley, Southsea
1942 Curls, Norwich; Bobbys, Exeter; Marshall & Snelgrove, Birmingham.

Badly damaged by enemy action were Bobbys at Bournemouth, and Wellsteeds, at Reading. Many lost sections of their premises. Windows were shattered, or blown in, from bombs detonating in nearby streets. At one stage, there was a daily procession of maintenance men, nailing up rolls of material, soaked in black pitch with supporting laths. Stock had to be rescued from mounds of rubble, and plaster frequently fell down, ruining goods. Bomb-damaged stock was cleared at sale prices and often stores bought the stock of others unable to resume trading, or helped to clear warehouses hit by fire and blast. Coping with it all were managers and an enlarging workforce of women. Overnight a street of shops could be transformed into an ugly series of ruins, divided by shops that had escaped. Suddenly a terraced building would find itself semi-detached and its interior walls exposed to view. Corrugated iron, black cars with hooded lights (and sometimes bags for gas to drive them), drab clothing and headscarves, were symbols of wartime life.

127

Bomb damage at Croydon

November 1940 was a black month. Enemy bombers struck again
Southampton, destroying much of the city centre, including the local Edwi
Jones store and the premises of Plummers. Out of the twisted girders an
concrete and brick rubble, stock was retrieved and materials saved. Withi
weeks, a large temporary building on part of the blitzed site was in use an
served throughout the remaining war years. When bombers raided Brist
and destroyed the Jones store, staff resourcefulness was soon evident.
snack bar in the Jones store was re-opened for business as a street kitche
with chef in white hat cheerfully stirring stew in a galvanized bath steamin
over an open fire. This immediate response to the needs of the moment s
impressed Miss Norma Bull, an Australian war correspondent, that sl
executed on the spot a water colour drawing of the incident.

On the night of 10 January 1941, Handleys of Southsea was devastated.
string of small shops was quickly acquired nearby and business resumed, b
they suffered constant damage, too. Repeated bombing of Plymouth in tl
spring of 1942 destroyed the Spooners store. Spooners' managing direct
(destined to become a future chairman of Debenhams) searched out altern;
tive property. 'Business As Usual' became a national slogan, even under tl
most makeshift and difficult conditions. Spooners had 34 shops in Plymout
and by the spring of 1941 all but ten had been destroyed. Almost as an act
bravado, Spooners erected a one-storey building in the heart of Plymouth
most devastated area. It survived and indeed traded until a new store cou
be opened in 1950. All Plymouth's big stores suffered from the terrifyin
concentration of high explosive on the city.

Curls at Norwich saw their premises shattered in April 1942. Buntings opposite was also destroyed. After the air raid, Curls established temporary premises by converting a nearby garage and warehouse, managing to open within a few weeks of the disaster a small departmental store. Curls also took over the basement of the local Garlands' premises, even re-establishing the noted Curls restaurant in its subsidiary's store.

In Debenhams' next incident, during May 1942, Bobbys' important store at Exeter exploded amid a shower of bricks and stock. The store occupied two separate buildings, with a church wedged between, and linked by an arcade. The church was spared even though the two Bobby buildings were lost. The whole of the Debenhams organization was vulnerable. Many acts of considerable courage and vigilance went unnoticed. Store fire-fighting teams developed great skills. Indeed, Kennards, the big Croydon store, was saved from batches of 30 incendiary bombs that fell across the roof and into nooks and crannies of its complex buildings.

War damage claims for all the ruin and destruction called for the most careful submissions by Debenhams estate and property experts. Some of the claims took not months but years to settle, but trade had to go on. When stores were ultimately rebuilt, the final cost considerably exceeded the amounts received from the War Damage Commission. This was to be expected for each store was rebuilt on a much larger and grander scale than before. Red tape was everywhere. The *Location of Retail Businesses Order* 1942, for example, stopped the opening of any new shops without a licence. This enabled stores suffering damage to get priority in re-establishing their trade without new competitors arriving to gain advantages.

*Kennards during the war
lecture on fuel saving*

WHAT THE PARACHUTE-MAN
MAY LOOK LIKE

Storekeeping became a question of survival and living with regulations. There was inventiveness and humour throughout it all. Driscoll at Croydon was particularly resourceful. He beat the blackout and lighting regulations by obtaining a quantity of luminous paint and splashing it around his dimly lit premises and proclaimed them to be the brightest spot in Croydon.

Improvisation was a test of managers, some of whom were inexperienced as many had gone into the armed forces. Women were given new responsibilities. Price controls were to be followed by clothes rationing, introduced in 1941. At first the allocation was 66 coupons a year and clothing was classed according to the yarn or fabric in an effort to determine relative values. Rationing lowered the quality of some goods, but in total war there had to be losses of standards. Fashion reflected the times. Common-sense clothing, particularly outerwear, was sold and women would add their own flourishes by plundering existing wardrobes for materials. Sewing machines came out to make garments from old dresses, and many woollen goods were unpicked and re-knitted, often for troops overseas.

In the middle of the war, the clothes ration was cut to 48 coupons a year. A man might obtain a shirt every two years, three pairs of socks every year, three pairs of shoes every two years, a pullover or waistcoat every five, and a two-piece suit every two. An overcoat would take seven years on the ration.

11 June
1942

The Hon: Unity Mitford
wuld like her jersey, for
which she has paid, to
be send to —

The Hon: Lady Mosley, 5433
Holloway Prison

London N7,
without a bill. She does not
know how many coupons,
so encloses Entire book.

Not everyone understood clothes rationing. An unusual and probably historic example can be found in a letter written by the Hon Unity Mitford friend of Hitler, to Ellistons store in Oxford on 11 June 1942. It says:

The Hon Unity Mitford would like her jersey, for which she has paid, to be send (sic) to – The Hon Lady Mosley 5433, Holloway Prison N7 without a bill. She does not know how many coupons, so encloses entire book.

Memories of wartime are numberless. Everyone who lived through the times has their favourite story. Larna Burbidge, a sales assistant with Bobbys, recalls brushing aside a junior to serve no less a person than Arthur Bobby, who presented his coupon book for a purchase. Mrs Burbidge thought the book was empty and detached the necessary coupons for the purchase, ripping it up before the puzzled Bobby. He moved away, looking back at her. Nervously, she re-checked and found she had actually torn up some unused coupons. They were stuck together and handed back with profuse apologies.

Mrs Cecilia Coomber captures something of the spirit on the home front in her own words:

It was a fine summer day in 1942. The doors of the store were opened wide to welcome Saturday afternoon shoppers. Then, without warning, enemy aircraft slipped through the defences and made a tip and run raid. My customers and I dropped behind a counter in a tangle of arms and legs when a bomb shook the foundations, hurling merchandise and plaster in all directions. After what seemed ages, it was all over. I looked round, no-one was hurt. The silence was heavy as I got to my feet and peered through a cloud of dust mingled with the acid smell of explosive. I looked towards the open door, and heard the steady clopping of footsteps approaching along the arcade to the store entrance. The customer entered, stepped over a mound of debris, spotted me behind the haberdashery counter, and said: 'Good afternoon, may I have two yards of white baby ribbon please.'

The introduction of the Utility scheme, which marked certain goods such as clothes and furniture with standard symbols, ensured that they had been made to certain specifications and guaranteed the quality and design. There were endless arguments among consumers as to whether utility goods were better than other products, but the scheme is now acknowledged as one of the great successes of wartime regulations. Today, more than a few homes still have utility furniture, with its distinctive trade symbol. The quality of manufacture can be seen on close inspection, despite timber shortages and war priorities.

Design of utility goods was functional and often inventive. The fussiness and waste of materials in designs that had been rooted in Victorian times was suddenly replaced by young ideas and clean lines. Designers looked anew at manufacturing processes and a new generation tried out concepts under the cover of officialdom, perhaps not immediately appreciated by consumers.

In the case of clothing, the utility scheme ensured a supply of garments of serviceable quality and at strictly observed low prices. Clothing was divided into utility and luxury. Dependable utility grades were intended to allay criticism that people with money would get the best. The utility mark became a symbol of acceptable quality and grumbles died away with trial and the long life of clothing that would not normally be expected to last. Many a man noticed that his utility socks lasted longer than the 'luxury' higher price pairs, which often had to be repaired with some ill-matching wool retrieved from a jumper.

Utility clothes were exempted from purchase tax, which had originally been seen by retailers as inflationary and an unnecessary restriction on consumers' choice to decide what were luxury items or not. Now men sat in Whitehall deciding what were essentials, semi-luxuries and luxuries. Purchase tax was riddled with anomalies, which persisted into peacetime, for Chancellors were loathe to abolish such a big revenue raising tax. Retailers were fed with streams of 'SROs and SIs', as they called the Government's regulations.

For women, the impact of war was severe. Years of unrelieved queuing for food, making do, home mending and darning, and coping with family tragedies did not make for good relations with some shopkeepers. The strain showed in later years, when constant cheerfulness began to give way to suspicions about cheating, under-the-counter dealings and other rumours. Family diets of Spam and Pom, exhortations on the radio from Lord Woolton's Ministry of Food to try some inedible recipe, and the greyness of street life, ought to have totally undermined their morale. Yet lives could be suddenly brightened. A lipstick snapped up at the local department store (cosmetics were short) could do wonders.

Women had their grapevines. They gathered on street corners and word of any stock of cosmetics at the department store could spread like wildfire. 'Have you heard ...?' was the opening gambit to many a march upon the local shops. All the well known brands of cosmetics fell into very short supply. Small amounts were released by the Board of Trade, and manufacturers' allocations favoured their best retailers. Smaller stores often went short and those lucky to receive some small deliveries only had limited quantities that vanished in under an hour when put on display. Substitutes became available from some new suppliers, and more than a few products were using materials of dubious origin and safety. Back kitchens were used to make products from chalk, stone and easily obtained substances. There were many cases of damage and injury to skin and lips. Women who eagerly purchased substitute face powders, lipsticks and creams began to do without.

Outside the utility schemes, manufacturers were permitted to produce items under what was called 'the general supplies category'. But the Board of Trade did not issue any licences to enable would-be manufacturers to obtain enough of the necessary materials. Shortages of cotton, rayon, wool, timber and the metals led to inventions of substitutes. In the fabric sector, raw materials came from rags and chopped up stockings. Timber substitutes were boards made from compressed straw, saw dust, and even paper.

One of the most common purchases for consumers was pot menders, metal discs with screw devices that covered holes as saucepans corroded and burnt out from excessive use. Stores and homes were stripped of surplus metal for the war effort and new pots and pans were always in short supply. Antique cooking pots were in much demand for their durability.

Staff problems were a constant worry for store managers. From 1940 onwards all able-bodied men went into the forces or onto war work. All single women were put to work, many being directed to essential war tasks in factories or on the land. Debenhams found its stores denuded of regular employees. Many married women were to be employed on a casual basis to cover the gaps. Most of these women had never before served in the retail trades and they became good employees, able to understand customers' problems.

All Debenhams executives who served during the war years say the trading results they achieved with a part-time labour force and the absence of trained people were very good. The assistants handled with great skill and fairness the queues that wound round department stores as some stock of nylon stockings, dress fabrics, sheets, towels or culinary ware became available. During this period, the manufacturing and wholesale business DLMS could only operate in a limited way, for it did not have any significant standing with manufacturers. Only a few Debenhams stores received the very scarce supplies that DLMS could obtain.

War brought new pressures on traders' attempts to survive shortage and bomb damage. Debenhams bought businesses and their allocations whenever they could. Between 1943 and 1945, the group acquired Jermyns of Kings Lynn, Griffin & Spalding of Nottingham, V. H. Bennett of Weymouth, E. P. Rose of Bedford, Dudleys of East London, and Stanleys of Birmingham. The Bobby group absorbed Simes of Worcester, Haymans of Totnes, and Dusts of Tunbridge Wells. Plummer Roddis took over premises in Andover, Bath, Southsea, and Yeovil, and renamed them. Morrish of Lewes was a typical purchase by Plummer. Kennards established its name over premises bought in Redhill and Staines. Not all these acquisitions were well judged, yet each had its supporting reasons.

Throughout these years, Debenhams was directed by Sir Frederick Richmond, and James Spence served as deputy chairman, with G. M. Wright as managing director. Spence's sons Tom and Jack served on the wartime board, as did C. J. L. Snowden and his son, L. C. Snowden.

The late thirties and early forties had a profound effect on department stores. From years of surging and exciting growth, from bargain basements and elephants advertising Jumbo clearance sales, the shops had to switch to controlled competition, regulations, rationing, and even physical devastation. Soldiers and others who returned to their jobs found Debenhams beset with problems, but it had survived war. Could it survive peace and changed attitudes?

7 Central buying

Our white Gandhi [Sir Stafford Cripps] is enforcing a crackpot plan to empty the shops at home in order to provide for shrinking, not to say, mythical markets abroad.

Brendan Bracken in a letter to Lord Beaverbrook, 11 November 1947

A leading management consultant, John Tyzack, once remarked: 'Management, like war, is made up of long periods of routine divided by short bursts of intense activity and peril.' It was an observation that might have been made with Debenhams in mind after the early post-war years brought together again executives and store staff to rebuild the business. Survival had to be secured by a combination of talents. War service brought a new perspective to more than a few young men and women. Then there was Fred Pope's class of 1930-39 – hard traders to a man, now returning to sit around tables with the older heads who had a sentimental regard for the grand old stores, often tolerating inefficiency and pleading the causes of personal service.

Success in rebuilding a business depended of course on people, whether in the boardroom, in executive suites, on sales floors, in stock rooms, or around the warehouses. Debenhams was not unlike other large concerns in that it grew out of many small businesses, which during the twenties amalgamated into considerable groups. These did not grow organically, like the chain stores. They were very much the result of complex financial negotiations and the resulting groupings required of their managements an ability to think on a large scale, while maintaining some of the entrepreneurial qualities of their founding fathers and even more ambitious succeeding generations.

Britain's recovery depended heavily on her businessmen and their capacity to develop home and export markets, yet a centrally planned economy threatened to hedge them round with new barriers to their freedom of decision. Retailers tended to be dynamic because they were close to the people, sensitive to their needs and aspirations in terms of living standards. Bankers were remote and dwelt in marble halls. Manufacturers had an arm's length relationship with consumers, paying third parties to research the public mind. Shopkeepers met the citizens every day, along with the milkman on Fridays and the bus conductor. More than a few businessmen had been thrown by war into close relationship with people from every walk of national life, and those who reflected on the experience were able to understand Britain's social transformation.

Retailing had not been exempt from the evolution of freedom for consumers, but what was ahead was nothing short of revolution. Shoppers were the pawns of retailers in wartime. In peace, and with victory, consumers wanted a rapid transition to stores full of new exciting fashion goods, plentiful food as well as secure employment providing decent wages, equal education, and homes. They watched the examples of choice and living standards set by the United States, but were prepared to try the new social order promised by economists and the political left.

In the event, they received Acts of nationalization and a prolonged period of further privation. Consumer demand was pent up, like a giant dam waiting to burst down upon the retail trades. Continued rationing was borne with a stoicism that belied the real frustration of people who wanted to rebuild their lives and enjoy material things, too.

A whole generation of wartime children received better education and their parents wanted to make up for their lost years. Restless and bewildered, the young men were conscripted in peacetime as national servicemen, perpetuating the mixing among people from homes of every income group.

A sensitivity to the social transformation of war, which brought people into an unaccustomed intimacy, was of paramount importance to any major company. The returning soldiers and a tired nation, in 1945, elected, by a landslide of votes, a Labour Government with a strong majority and big plans, but with a bankrupted Exchequer. Recovery from war brought its misery and unfulfilled promises to the people, particularly consumers. Cripps and austerity constrained the natural instincts of any shoppers with more money to spend. Freedom from war was replaced by extended controls and persistent shortages. Bitter winters, made worse by coal shortages, and continued rationing, sapped enthusiasm for Socialism. Profiteers moved in on war surplus goods and black markets reared criminals, termed 'spivs' and 'wide boys'. A National Health Service gave tremendous impetus to the emergence from war of a restless yet homogeneous and egalitarian generation.

Attempts to restore distinctions of class and social status, reflected by some of the first films made by the revived British film industry, were doomed. People wanted to escape into the celluloid world depicted by Hollywood, where Joe the petrol pump attendant drove a big car, and his wife could be seen pushing a strange wheeled basket in what looked like Aladin's Cave, filling the wire trolley with packaged foods of every description.

The immediate years of peace were to see store managers and their buyers engaged in a mad scramble to find stocks of goods for people who felt an urge to spend. Savings were being released and soldiers had gratuities and back pay. Fred Besley, later a managing director of Debenhams, recalls running the store at Great Yarmouth. While beaches were being cleared of mines and anti-invasion devices, he scoured warehouses for stocks of surplus goods. Holiday camps, hotels, and guest houses were being restored. Customers would watch freight arrivals at the local station and rush to the store to see what was subsequently on offer. Army surplus goods came from Northern Ireland. Blocks of clothing coupons were exchanged in deals with the holiday caterers. Besley said:

Selling was easy. It was finding stock which became the important factor. Our buyers travelled everywhere, and at Yarmouth we doubled our trade for several years as a result of their ingenuity. Boots, materials, socks, parachute silk, cutlery, pots and pans – you name it, we found it.

People also wanted to satisfy a hunger to express themselves. That was why fashion goods and cosmetics were now in such demand by women. The 'New Look' raised false expectations that the days of skimping on clothing materials and design were quickly passing. Fashion had been very much a privilege of the wealthy, but manufacturers had learned in wartime the benefits of productivity derived from long production runs. Their first post-war garments, nonetheless, lacked colour and style.

Clearly new fashions had to be taken to the masses. The population wanted light, colourful and comfortable clothing. They wanted products requiring easy care and new washing qualities. Nylon, developed before the war, was in great demand. These were requirements seen quickly by Marks & Spencer, Debenhams, and others, but each store group reacted in varying ways. Debenhams was caught between decisions to restore London stores to their former status while exploiting mass demand for more fashionable textiles through an entrenched position in many provincial High Streets.

As a group, Debenhams was vulnerable to the scientific management techniques being pioneered by Marks & Spencer, which shed its pre-war ideas at break-neck speed and organized suppliers through a stream of orders based on rigid specifications. Department stores were open to attack from all quarters. There were 1200 variety chain stores hungry for trade, and the Coop was then powerful, running its own factories. Tailoring for the masses was reflected in the Montague Burton and Weaver-to-Wearer organizations.

In wartime, department stores had held one-seventh of women's and children's wear sales, nearly 20 per cent of all furniture and furnishing purchases, and an eighth of the hardware, pottery, glass and ironmongery trades. Multiples and cooperative societies tried to assail their trade as never before and, given the controlled growth in overall retail expenditure, competition had to be unremitting.

The killing had stopped. Now a shopping revolution which transformed every High Street in Britain was about to begin. It started slowly enough. A small procession of shopkeepers sailed the Atlantic to study self-service retailing methods in the United States. Trade journals reported new American ideas in running department stores, full of scientific jargon, plus details of the latest in layouts and stock control systems.

Although there was always a waiting list for permits to travel the Atlantic, executives from Debenhams brought back periodic reports on the startling progress made in the United States, whose wealth and mass production methods had been maintained despite wartime alliances and commitments. Europe was in chaos, supported by loans and aid. British shopkeepers returned from visits to see the latest in department stores or brash supermar-

kets run on self-selection lines with conflicting recommendations on th
implications for retailing.

It is astonishing to read in contemporary records and reports the consider
able scepticism about transplanting American methods and ideas. Self
service shopping was consequently left to a few pioneers in the food trade
who stole an early post-war lead over competitors with their counters, old
fashioned aproned counter hands, and dusty premises. Packaging and pre
sentation were more important to Americans than home delivery. Ever
supplier of a new consumer product was to be encouraged. Americans wer
uninhibited and her 160 million people were an unparallelled self-sufficier
market, fostering innovation and highly productive manufacturing.

British retailers were but poor relations. More than a few regarded wit
horror the newer bright shops of the United States, with flexible fixtures an
fittings and goods in pre-packed transparent wrappings or boxes. The
wanted no part in emulating American shopkeepers, who mirrored a quit
different society where a friendly people worked hard and expected to b
rewarded with the highest standard of living in a world which their mone
was now helping to safeguard. Nevertheless, American store layouts an
merchandising methods attracted admiring comment from those younge
men who stayed in retailing when others left after the war for factories an
manufacturing companies.

In the higher reaches of Debenhams, Americana was an alien culture
Visiting US suppliers and investors in Britain were keen to do business whe
quotas and allocations eased. Yet they were regarded, frequently, as figure
of fun. Men with Texan accents or Brooklyn drapers were, nonetheless
master salesmen and ready to embrace every new idea in their search fo
those extra dollars of business. They had spawned, with the help of Madiso

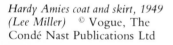

*Hardy Amies coat and skirt, 1949
(Lee Miller)* © Vogue, The
Condé Nast Publications Ltd

Avenue, markets for home appliances, packaged and refrigerated goods, and catered for millions of car owning shoppers.

In 1948 and into the fifties, a war-weary Britain continued to queue at cinemas to see the latest films which gave glimpses of life styles and homes filled with goods to which they aspired. A few hours in a dimly lit cinema was an escape to America's other world, where kitchens were fitted with giant refrigerators bulging with food, and women were glamorous. The envy of British consumers was to grow. Feelings about the drabness of early post-war products and all the shortages grew into a potent political force. People did not just want factories, hospitals, and schools. They wanted good shops which cared for their needs. Labour's Festival of Britain in 1951 and the later bonfires of controls and ration books by Conservatives, when returned to power, restored shoppers' confidence.

The housewives also voted with their shopping baskets, pouring into the early self-service shops and patronizing the chain stores which threw out old ideas of service.

Department stores found themselves in a quandary. On the one hand, the established multiples and chain stores were beginning to become well financed by institutional money, taking advantage of every relaxation of building control or town centre redevelopment to modernize and to increase their presence in main shopping areas. On the other, newcomers to retailing, some reared from the nursery of street markets, were buying up leases of small- and medium-sized shops at bargain rentals.

Trade had to be won in competition with such organizations. Retail sales grew slowly at first in overall terms, so volume had to be gained at the expense of each other. A prime target for any business of size had to be the big share of national trade held by independent shopkeepers – some 60 per

Kennards of Croydon dressed for the Coronation, 1953

cent in 1950 when the first Census of Distribution was taken. Britain ha
around 700 department stores, each employing more than twenty-fi
people. Excluding the Coop's 200, there were around 500 in ownership
families or publicly quoted groups with a combined labour force of 130 000

There were over a dozen groups operating more than five stores each ar
between them they controlled, in 1950, nearly 140 department stores wir
total sales over £130m. The average sales of such stores stagnated in the ne
seven years (sales value went up only 27 per cent against a 53 per cent for a
retail trade in the same period).

As the biggest departmental store group in Britain, Debenhams no
comprised eighty-four companies with 110 stores and assets of £36m. Yet i
issued capital had remained at £6.2 million since reorganization in 1934. I
1948, as one of his last acts, Sir Frederick Richmond capitalized reserves ar
reconstructed the issued share capital, enlarging it to £7.7m. Two years late
the chairman heeded medical advice and resigned. His sixty-two years c
trading had spanned the transition of Debenhams' family partnership to tl
creation of a major public company, and in his final year seven retail busine
ses were bought.

The new chairman was G. M. Wright, strong on finance and more
home wheeling and dealing in stocks of a paper kind. Old habits die har
And Wright was soon juggling the accounts, looking for funds for tl
modernization which Pope and others urged upon him. Wise or not, Wrigl
forced through the sale of stores in the Scottish Drapery Corporation, i
which Debenhams had a substantial but not a majority holding, to Hug
Fraser, the Scottish draper. With stores spreading from Aberdeen to Gla
gow and Edinburgh, this deal was to enable the Fraser Group to develc
even bigger ambitions. Wright pushed up Debenhams share capital agaiı
after the deal, by capitalization of reserves to £10.7m.

The rising star within Debenhams was John Bedford, who had served
long apprenticeship around the group, running stores in Birminghan
Plymouth, and the East Coast. Under G. M. Wright's chairmanshiʝ
Debenhams had to bridge the past with the present and Bedford, who wa
made joint managing director, had sufficient old school style to bring
maturity to his many new ideas. The ill health of Wright's deputy, R. I
Gaze, brought, in 1954, the deputy chairmanship to Bedford, enhancing h
authority.

Between Sir Frederick Richmond's retirement in 1950 and Bedford
promotion to deputy chairman, the directors pushed on with store rede
velopment, buying up new businesses whenever they were offered. Still the
came into the group – Prettys of Bury St Edmunds, Adnitts of Northamʝ
ton, Bradleys of Chepstow Place, Affleck & Brown, of Manchester, Ellisto
& Cavell of Oxford, Thornton-Varley of Hull, and Farmers of Nottinghan
It was not all plain sailing. Heaps of Bury was to be sold off, while Pendle
burys of Wigan was burnt down.

Pendleburys had been bought in 1949, along with two other Norwic
concerns, (Buntings and Chamberlin), deals which were somewhat over
shadowed by the purchase of Woollands of Knightsbridge.

The Bedford years, as they became known to executives, began on

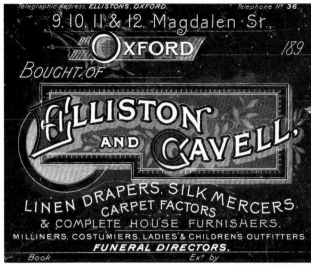

bright note – the opening of the rebuilt Handley's store at Southsea. Splashing out on buying up small family concerns was one thing, but re-opening war-shattered, or out-of-date, stores was another. Protracted negotiations with local authorities had disrupted the rate of profits when competitors outside the department store sector were attracting stock market praise. As shoppers crowded into Handleys, major new store developments were under construction at Plymouth, Bristol, Southampton, Norwich, and Birmingham.

In 1956 there was a change at the top, for Wright finally relinquished the chairmanship. He had six months to live. Bedford began quietly enough, taking over Leas of Leicester and presiding over the re-openings of Marshall & Snelgrove in Birmingham, and Spooners down in Plymouth.

Bedford had originally been earmarked for the law but ended up as a retailer with twenty-five years' experience within Debenhams. He had a

long experience of looking over businesses offered to Debenhams and had been brought to London in 1949 by Sir Frederick Richmond to examine the problem of utilizing Debenhams' dissipated buying power.

It appeared to Bedford that the group had grown without rhyme or reason and the requirement was to harness its vast buying power in a way that met competition at every point, whether in the higher class stores or in the popular stores outside London. Debenhams was a conglomerate of other names. The company's name meant nothing to the shopper at Plummer Roddis in Guildford or Griffin & Spalding in Nottingham.

Many a young executive had pointed out that the individual stores still had considerable autonomy, going their own way. Some had differing reputations. Garlands in Norwich had a big name for fashions, but sister stores in the city trading under the names Curls, Chamberlins, and Buntings were noted for expertise in other departments. Everyone was, of course, now looking to Bedford for leadership, and the new chairman allowed debate to develop over the merits of bigger and better planned buying that would impact on the competition from chain stores and others. There was little centralized buying in the world of department stores, though the John Lewis Partnership had pioneered changes.

What was evident to Bedford and his advisers was that it was becoming more difficult to find and to train buyers for smaller stores. Great expertise and skill were needed. The difference between profits and losses often rested on successful judgements. DLMS was pointing a way, though impetus was lost with the death of F. J. Pope, the master of popular trade.

Debenhams was riddled with committees of barons drawn from the individual stores, with their various classifications within which there were other tiers. Even popular stores varied in style and merchandising methods

Pauldens of Manchester on fire, 1957

Gradually, the best buyers were floating to the top of liaison committees ordering the limited range of goods picked for pilot schemes upon which central buying might be based. Fred Besley was among the advocates of bulk buying and he watched the turmoil created by the early attempts to coordinate operations. Not until Besley was given the chairmanship of the 'C' group of Debenhams stores did things start to happen.

He persuaded the various chairmen that control of bought ledgers had to pass increasingly to the centre. This was the age of the computer, increasingly being introduced into stock control in retailing, and vigorous price competition. The days of cosy margins flowing from resale price maintenance by suppliers were numbered.

The internal debate over central buying raged on. A three-day conference at Eastbourne, when talks were fierce and sustained, broken only by golf and dinners, revealed the extent of feelings. It became very clear to Besley that he would 'carry the can' if things went badly awry.

Whether or not it was right for Bedford to let debate flare and executives squabble remains a matter for argument to this day. But what seems important is that he sensed the need for reforms. He had fought an unnecessary battle with Wright over the eventual introduction, in 1957, of a group contributory pension scheme, long overdue and made possible by profits earned on the sale of the Scottish Drapery Corporation. Bedford had properties revalued and raised more capital.

Between 1957 and 1959, Bedford acquired Taylors of Bristol, the Edward Grey group in Birmingham, Ranbys of Derby, Busbys of Bradford and Harrogate, Corders of Ipswich, Stones of Romford, and Chapmans of Taunton. A huge fire destroyed Pauldens main store in Manchester, blunting the satisfaction of the rebuilding and opening of Pendleburys (burnt down in Wigan several years before) or the handsome new Jones store in Bristol. There was innovation. The first of several experimental dry goods supermarkets was opened within Kennards of Croydon under the name of 'Welbeck'.

Potentially exciting to younger executives was the acquisition of Cresta

143

Silks, a small group of retail fashion shops said to have great potential.

Cresta was under the control of Eric Crabtree, a solicitor with moder ideas for winning sales from what he called the Rover-driving plutocracy of the shires and industrial towns who wanted stylish dresses at keen price with plenty on the racks for selection. Crabtree had previously been join managing director of Berketex, the dress manufacturers who pioneere shops-within-shops. When the Trust bought Cresta Silks (founded by th Heron family and specialists in fabrics, operating with fifteen shops), Crab tree was able to obtain control. After the Debenhams take-over, Bedford le Crabtree to run things, giving him the feeling the business was still his own

Crabtree's ability to buy centrally and to market clothes for the afflue women at prices, and with a range of choice, often better than departme stores, only added fuel to the argument within Debenhams about centr buying. The appointment of four relatively young men in 1958 to th Debenhams main board seemed to point to fundamental change. Up to th time, the policy was for each director, except those centred on London wit administrative functions, to be chairmen of groups of businesses, as well serving as managing directors of the principal stores within each grou Now the main board seemed fully representative of nearly every subsidiary

There had to be changes. Fred Besley, who became managing directo recalls the painful process. He began a long internal argument about wheth Marshall & Snelgrove in Oxford Street should be renamed Debenhams, move designed to achieve 'a less class image', but not acted upon until 197 More to the point was the argument that, if central buying was to succee there had to be more uniformity. A first move was to indicate to shoppe that their local department store was controlled by Debenhams, and windo boards began appearing declaring the various premises to be 'A Debenha Store'. For millions of shoppers this came as a surprise – the carefully nu tured image of family-owned and run stores was deeply rooted in man localities. The point hammered home by Besley and others in hours discussion was that central buying was easy, given sufficient expertise an capital. The art was to sell the merchandise. Yet there was no point adverti ing a Debenhams offer nationally or pushing new brand names unless cu tomers knew the stores to go to. Experiments with Debenhams advertise ments, filled with long lists of stores with equally long names, were doome to failure. Buying in bulk required selling in bulk, whether footwear, a early trial, or electrical goods, such as 4000 domestic refrigerators boug from LEC and cleared in a dramatic demonstration of the advantages.

The switch to central buying and the development of brand names prove to be a long, long process. And it was disrupted by another battle whi diverted management attention at this critical time.

8 In the bear garden

Lord Fraser of Allander

*I do not like take-over bids, and I
do not like the people who make them.*

John Bedford,
Chairman of Debenhams, 1956-71

It was with these words that John Bedford, on 28 August 1959, ended three turbulent months during which Debenhams found itself plunged into a bear garden, fighting a rival draper Mr Hugh Fraser, later knighted then ennobled as Lord Fraser of Allander, for control of the Harrods group of stores. Fraser was among a breed of post-war individuals whose names were associated with a spate of share offers in the fifties: men such as Clore, Samuel, Wolfson, and Sunley. Take-overs were as old as business in general, but in 1959 they had become set pieces on the City stage, for that year there were ninety-eight public companies involved in a series of merger deals and 461 private companies became embroiled in negotiations, some friendly, some not.

In its way, Debenhams was a gentle whale swallowing smaller fish. It was not a natural predator and even firms which were acquired were allowed to retain their identities and family management in return for capital and a few seats on their boards. Yet the summer of 1959 saw Debenhams engaged in a bitter struggle for control of Harrods, which became a classic for study by students of the post-war phenomenon of growth by mergers and sudden bids for shares.

The irony of the struggle for Harrods was that Debenhams had encouraged the rise of Hugh Fraser seven years before by disposing of the Scottish Drapery Corporation to the then four-year-old House of Fraser, a public company created out of Fraser Sons & Company, formed in 1875 but traceable back to the original retail drapery business established in Glasgow in 1849.

Fraser amalgamated the Scottish Drapery Corporation's stores with fifteen retail stores he already controlled in Edinburgh and Glasgow. In 1953, his House of Fraser crossed the border and captured nine Binns stores in the North-East of England. Four years later he marched into London, buying the major department store group of John Barker & Co, giving him control of Barkers, Pontings, Derry & Toms and Zeeta, as well as Muirheads.

Hardy Amies in the late fifties
Left to right: *Workrooms Fit-*
ting Design conference Showing

Besides Debenhams, whose total assets at £56m compared with £28m for Fraser, the leading departmental stores groups by 1959 were Harrods (including Dickins & Jones, D. H. Evans, Kendal Milne, Wm. Henderson, and Rackhams), the John Lewis Partnership (John Lewis, Peter Jones, John Barnes, Tyrrel & Green, and Waitrose supermarkets), and the Lewis's Investment Trust (Lewis's and Selfridges). This, then, was the setting for the battle with Fraser which was to follow.

For the City, 19 June 1959 was another day dominated by bid fever. Charles Clore's Sears dropped their bid for Watney Mann, the brewers, but before the day was over Hugh Fraser revealed from his Glasgow headquarters that he had made a merger proposal to Sir Richard Burbidge, chairman of Harrods. Harrods' shares jumped on the news, but Burbidge kept his silence until a board meeting scheduled for Monday, 22 June 1959.

Take-over rumours had beset Harrods several times in the previous few years, but Sir Richard more than once declared a preference for independence. News of Fraser's move galvanized Debenhams and the week-end saw Bedford busy on the telephone and making contacts. John Bedford was being forced to revise his policy, for he said: 'All Debenhams acquisitions have been on the basis of willing buyer and willing seller.'

Harrods would make a major acquisition for either group. For Debenhams the combined group would be incomparably the largest department store group in the country. A merger with the House of Fraser, on the other hand, would bring a serious rival to Debenhams.

There were, of course, considerations other than just size. For years the numbers of independent department stores had been declining. Eighteen months before it had been calculated that there were only about twenty independent department stores left with a turnover of more than £1m a year, and the number had continued to shrink.

Among the reasons which had compelled amalgamations and invited take-overs, the first was the rise in site values, often inadequately reflected in

146

balance sheet values. The golden age of developing department stores was the period 1880–1914. Most sites and many buildings dated from then. Secondly, the fact that so many department stores were family businesses which grew from small drapers' shops meant that death duties hit them particularly hard. Many were to be found at the heart of prosperous shopping centres, in the creation of which they had played a leading part. Expansion on the original site became difficult or impossible, so that when successful stores wished to expand, often the only way was by acquiring existing businesses.

Yet it was by no means clear how many real economies resulted from department store mergers. Theoretically, it should be possible to effect large savings by enlargement of buying power and larger trade discounts. One of the main disadvantages that department stores suffered in contrast with the specialist chains was that their buying power was comparatively so small. But the higher the class of business the store transacted the more important individuality in merchandise became and the smaller the scope for this kind of economy.

Moreover, integration could run into all kinds of snags. If there was some local buying as well as a central buying organization, administration costs were higher. If local buyers had to accept central merchandise, it was all too easy for them to make no real effort to sell it. If reorganization was sufficiently ruthless to ensure compliance, the character of the shop might suffer, while, if control was merely financial, expense ratios might not be significantly reduced.

In a pertinent comment, the *Financial Times* said:

In this connection it is notable that Debenhams, whose stores range from 'high class' to 'popular', has been seeking to expand the popular end of its business, where the scope for standardization is greatest. It has also been engaged in vertical integration and has introduced a number of its own brand names. The move on its part to join with Harrods thus seems a step away from this policy.

Behind these problems was the fact that there was a shadow over the future of department stores. Their failure since the war to keep pace with the multiples in expansion was a cause for City comment. In the years between 1950 and 1957 their total share of retail trade dropped from 6 to about 5 per cent, while the multiples' share went up from 23 per cent to 25 per cent or more. With wages representing on occasion some two-thirds of department store costs, the services they offered customers seemed bound to become an increasing burden.

These factors had even led to suggestions that the department stores, or at any rate their present standards of service and choice, were doomed. It was significant that Harrods had sailed through the difficult post-war years with its standards unimpaired.

Harrods was a group in whose crown was the great jewel represented by its world-famous store in Knightsbridge, hard by the Debenhams group's Harvey Nichols and Woollands.

Harrods began in 1849, when Henry Charles Harrod bought a small grocery shop at No. 8 Middle Queen's Buildings (later part of Brompton Road).

The grocery shop enjoyed a fair trade in those early days when Knightsbridge was becoming something of a fashionable quarter under the stimulus of the great exhibition of 1851 in Hyde Park. Ten years later, when it was taken over by the owner's son, Charles Digby Harrod, the business began to expand rapidly. Young Harrod, when he first took control of the shop, placed his nameplate in front of the wire blind in the window. In 1873 he was acquiring the leases of adjoining premises in Brompton Road, which he faced with plate glass, and above the windows the name 'Harrod's Stores' appeared. The business grew until 1883 when, less than three weeks before Christmas, the buildings and stocks were destroyed by fire. A large iron structure in Brompton Road known as Humphrey's Hall was used as a temporary shop and within four days business was being carried on as usual. In spite of the fire the Christmas trade was a record.

The premises were rebuilt within a year of the fire, and many new departments were added to the store. Charles Harrod decided to retire in 1889 and formed the business into a company with a capital of £141 400. There followed a drop in trade which was so alarming that Harrod was asked to return and keep the business going until another general manager could be found. In 1891 the first Richard Burbidge became manager, and Harrod retired to enjoy a country life until he died in 1905.

From this time until the war in 1914 the store enjoyed almost uninterrupted prosperity. By 1901 the company had acquired all the leases necessary to enable it to start building on an island site, and the premises, as they are today, began to rise. Three years before, in 1898, the first escalator was installed and was much commented on in the newspapers. By 1914 the firm had nearly 6000 people in its employment, and the annual turnover was almost £4m.

The acquisition in 1973 of the Army and Navy followed the purchases of Dickins & Jones and D. H. Evans. Expansion was undertaken in Manchester and big plans existed for Birmingham, when battle was joined between the Fraser and Bedford camps.

There was no doubt that, over the week-end of 20 and 21 June, Bedford felt confident that his friendly discussions with Sir Richard Burbidge would halt Fraser's ambitions. On the Monday morning, the Harrods directors met and unanimously recommended acceptance of an offer from Debenhams which put a value of £34 500 000 on the Knightsbridge enterprise. The £1 shares of Harrods were valued at £6. 10s. by the offer of four 10 shillings Ordinary Debenham shares against Fraser's 20s. cash and some A shares.

'It seems hardly fair,' Fraser told the *Financial Times* angrily when he heard the decision. At no time during his talks with Harrods had he received any indication that a rival offer might be made. Fraser had originally approached Harrods on 9 June 1959, but had been kept waiting.

Harrods saw its future with Debenhams because the group's interests would, according to Sir Richard, 'continue as separate entities carrying on their traditional type of business'. By merging, there would be an exchange of directorships to the benefit of the shopping public.

Far from retiring, Fraser decided to fight on. Share registers divulged that big institutions and nominees ranging from the Alliance to the Cooperative Insurance held big blocks of shares. Such investors would sense a struggle in which they would hang onto shares, surrendering them as the values went up. He came from a different school from Bedford when it came to take-over situations.

While Fraser, whose first offer limited voting rights, went into a huddle with his advisers, there came a dramatic development as share values soared on the Stock Exchange in expectation of counter offers. On 25 June, United Drapery Stores, owning more than 750 shops, offered to buy Harrods with a £36m bid – some £3m higher than Debenhams and certainly more than preparations by Fraser to match Debenhams pound for pound. Sir Richard called another board meeting as the City sat back to await developments.

Moves came thick and fast. First, Fraser decided to enfranchise his A stockholders, reorganizing capital and meeting criticism of the use of non-voting shares. In the House of Commons, Mr (now Sir) Harold Wilson observed that Harrods were not even playing hard to get. Nonetheless, the Harrods directors decided to make no public comment until they received all the formal offers from the three suitors. For his part, Fraser clearly had to outbid both Debenhams and United Drapery, whose intervention reduced the chance of the former's success.

The Harrods directors did not want Fraser in control and, as they had indicated this by so swiftly favouring Debenhams, the UDS bid at least enabled them to reject Fraser while taking account of rising share values, in which stockholders were vitally interested. Clearly, the struggle was now not about benefits to shoppers and trading policy, but about shareholders and the profits to be made from a take-over struggle.

Early in July, Fraser slapped down on the Harrods boardroom table a new offer worth £37m in shares and cash. To support this fourth offer facing the Harrods directors, Fraser had been buying shares in the market. The fact that he had to find large amounts of cash to finance the deal did not bother the market, into which UDS had gone to snap up shares, too. Debenhams took counsel from its merchant bank advisers, Lazards, for Fraser's tactics included a complicated revision of his detailed offers for Preference and Ordinary shares, designed to give him early voting control of enough Ordinary shares.

To back up his offers, Fraser revealed plans to raise funds from Barker properties, either by sales or by mortgages. Shareholders became nervous as market values began to fall by the end of the month. Fraser made himself readily available to the financial press, while Debenhams kept a tactful silence.

The silence was broken on 28 July 1959, when Debenhams counterattacked, raising its bid to £37m. Debenhams directors stated: 'We still believe that those who invest in, deal with or work for Debenhams and Harrods would have much to gain if the two groups of businesses were brought together.'

Confronted with this determination, the UDS board threw in the towel. It was now a straight fight between Debenhams and Fraser, with the former relying on a superior bid for Harrods Preference shares. The Harrods directors unanimously supported the Debenhams offer, but Fraser seized an advantage by rushing to UDS to buy a big block of Harrods shares, giving itself 15 to 20 per cent of Harrods votes. Shares had been offered by UDS to Debenhams, but its directors turned them down – a fatal mistake – because they were offered on terms higher than in the formal offer.

The struggle now took a new and decisive turn, as Fraser splashed out on more Ordinary shares. There was some criticism of Debenhams on the grounds that it would have to increase its capital because the bid for Harrods was too high. This stung Bedford. He explained his attitude to the *Financial Times*:

We examine all the offers that are made to us, and when we have felt that the price was too high we have declined the offer. We were recently asked to pay 45s. for the United Drapery's Preference shareholding in Harrods, and declined not only because we were not prepared to make one bid in public and another in private, but felt that the price was too high.

In the past few years it has been the practice of Debenhams to acquire other businesses in the trade and by greater efficiency and economies we have steadily increased the trading profits of the Group. This record I think justifies me in saying that I and my co-directors have had considerable experience of the type of business and profitability which would fit in best with Debenhams. We now believe that closer cooperation between our Group and Harrods should bring considerable advantages both to shareholders and customers.

Paper warfare continued, with stockbrokers issuing circulars of varying quality on how shareholders, yet to commit themselves, should decide between the improved offers from both sides. Opinion was shifting towards Debenhams, and in mid-August the influential Lex column in the *Financial Times* urged its case. The apparent success was short-lived – for on 17 August Fraser raised his offer to £38m to which Debenhams replied by a letter restating the logic of its own merger proposals. It was talk, not cash but Bedford was angry with a Fraser circular which claimed it was a better performer on profits than Debenhams.

Bedford took advertisements explaining that such comparisons were misleading for the period 1948 to 1958. In the first seven years of this period, Debenhams was rebuilding six of the ten largest and most profitable stores which had been destroyed by enemy action and repairing no less than thirty which were damaged. Harrods shareholders taking Debenhams 'paper' could be better covered, for what mattered in business was the future ability to raise profits. But shareholders wanted more than words, and on 19 August the Debenhams board revised their offer to £38m, but because of its mixture of cash and paper Fraser called Bedford's new broadside a 'damp squib', and said his offer stood.

The City held its breath. Would this be stalemate? 21 August was the day of decision, for those who had not yet accepted one or other of the rival bids now had to choose. At the last moment, market sentiment was moving in favour of Fraser, while more than a few people were impressed by Fraser's dynamic personality and unsure about Bedford, a figure not well known to many people. They were being faced with a choice of throwing their lot in with the conservative Debenhams, or the heady expansionism envisaged by Fraser. Into post boxes around Britain and in the City, shareholders expressed their preference.

When Fraser boarded an aircraft on 23 August for a holiday in Monte Carlo, he claimed he had received enough acceptances of his offer to obtain control. Whether it was bluff or not, more acceptances came in. It was all over bar the final counting. The fight had turned both on the relative value of the shares and the fact that Fraser had proved readier to pay cash as well as in paper.

Debenhams withdrew from the struggle on 24 August, bitter and wiser. Bedford commented:

We started off on a friendly basis with a straightforward merger. It was only the intervention of other people that turned it into a bear garden. I do not like take-over bids, and I do not like the people who make them.

The beaten Bedford stressed that having got Debenhams involved he did not feel the directors could withdraw. They made no deals in the market above offer prices. Debenhams could have won had Bedford adopted certain methods, but 'with the reputation of Debenhams in mind I was not prepared to do that'.

There was a certain irony in the whole affair. Fraser had triumphed over Bedford with smaller resources and against the advice of the Harrods board. One mistake by Debenhams was to put a closing date on its offer which fell after the Fraser date. The *Financial Times* said Fraser left an impression of superior determination and a willingness to do anything to gain control of Harrods. The irony was that when it came to adding up the cost to Debenhams, not in dented reputations but money, the group had emerged from defeat with a small profit – £17 077, after covering expenses of the battle and disposing of its own package of Harrods shares through the market.

For Fraser the ownership of Harrods brought prestige. He was to live another seven years, dying as a peer and concentrating on his other major interest, Scottish and Universal Investments. His son, Sir Hugh, did not lack ambition and the House of Fraser resumed take-overs between 1969 and 1973, buying up store groups in Grimsby, Belfast, Bournemouth, Hull, Cardiff, and Plymouth. Fraser swallowed the Baird Group and then over-reached itself in 1974 with a spectacular merger deal involving the Boots Company. The Monopolies Commission said it should not be permitted.

By that time, Debenhams was back in the bear garden, though this time displaying a skill in City tactics which the late Lord Fraser would have openly admired. It was, however, a question of survival, for this time Debenhams felt what it was like to be the prey against a predator.

There can be no doubt that Bedford and his board took a severe knock, though history must judge the correctness of their decisions, which have a ring of honour. They could have bought the UDS shareholding at a price, discriminating between shareholders, and probably won.

In defeat, Debenhams plunged itself into another programme of new building and rationalization. A footwear division was created, merging shop-in-shop services provided from Gloucester and Southampton to fifty other group stores. It was another step towards central buying. There were even more acquisitions: Newhouse in Middlesbrough, Bonds in Chelmsford, Tuttles in Lowestoft, and even Peal & Co. in London's Burlington Arcade. The fourteen-branch business, Leaders Fashions, was added to the ever-growing list (joining Cresta), which also included manufacturers.

H. J. Ward, a Nottingham garment house, and the Fine Gauge Hosiery Co. were bought up, the latter to make stockings under the Golden Dawn label being promoted by Debenhams. Overseas, the picture was different, as wholesale branches closed one by one.

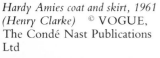

Hardy Amies coat and skirt, 1961 (Henry Clarke) © VOGUE, The Condé Nast Publications Ltd

And so the procession continued. Buying businesses is easy, given sufficient capital. Operating them at a profit is another consideration, even if each new member of Debenhams brought in more turnover to disguise the rate of gains in sales in real terms. Nothing seemed too big or too small. In 1961 a small removal firm Wort & Son was bought for the Harvey Nichols Removals subsidiary in Bournemouth, and the year also brought in the small Guildford chain called Gammans.

Another year of patient reforms passed. In 1962, Debenhams decided to acquire the outstanding minority interests in twenty-six subsidiary companies in the Debenham group, and this covered thirty-six different classes of capital.

There was yet another acquisition – the Matthias Robinson group of stores at Leeds, Stockton, West Hartlepool, and Darlington. Work progressed on new stores, notably the new Nicholsons store in Bromley. This company had been forced to close their store in the City of London, due to the replanning proposals for the St Paul's Churchyard area. The Bromley development was a novel project, for Debenhams bought a cinema and converted it to a department store.

By now Debenhams was deeply involved in national advertising, making use of such house brand names as 'Debroyal' and 'Golden Dawn'. The name of 'Welsmere' had begun to appear too. Fred Besley was not letting up on central buying and promotion.

Apart from the opening of the new Nicholsons store, 1963 was a 'black year'. There now began rationalization with many store closures. L. C. Snowden, a managing director of Debenhams, was appointed deputy chairman, making way for Fred Besley and J. R. Dixon as joint managing directors. The chairman was also a managing director.

Stores now opened and closed everywhere. In 1964 Debenhams acquired John Yeo's of Plymouth, whose store was adjacent to Spooners.

Annual reports and brochures were filled with pictures of steelwork, scaffolded premises, and new stores. Staff were given a five-day working week. The stores of Rowntrees of York went on the balance sheet. An administrative headquarters where computers could control bought ledgers and provide instant buying data was set up at Taunton under the name Bedford House.

Rebuilding came to Stones of Romford, Chapmans of Taunton, and Bobbys of Worcester. The directors began paying increasing attention to the laggards in the organization, which were not trading on a sufficiently profitable basis to justify the use of their assets, especially the land on which they stood. Premises of Kennards of Redhill, Chamberlins of Norwich, and Gardiner at Ipswich were sold. Subsequently, the businesses in London of Staddons, Dawson Bros. (London) and Z. Dudley were sold. These were in the credit and club type of trading, and somewhat alien to the Debenham organization. Three new stores were ordered for Bobbys of Exeter, Pauldens of Sheffield, and Plummer Roddis in Guildford.

When full-scale central buying commenced, initial work covered the purchasing (the bought ledger), and all the stores' invoices and statements were sent to Taunton for action. An initial arrangement was made to 'hire time'

The new store at Romford

on computers around the country, to cope with the flood of invoices and statements, and the related paperwork connected with those activities. Debenhams next moved their registrar's department out of Wimpole Street to Taunton, followed by DLMS transferring their financial administration, too. Later would come Debenhams' own computer installation.

Other reforms were becoming urgent. The insularity of Debenhams was causing comment in the City and the financial press. Investors wanted growth and a performance which matched that to be found in other sectors of retailing. Results could not, however, be won without painful reappraisal. Modernization took time. Few casual investors had the patience to see that Debenhams, late as it was with national merchandising and stock control, was looking above and beyond the immediate future. Improved results would come, given time, promised faithful executives when pressed to explain some poor results or to answer the progress of others.

For his part John Bedford, as chairman, pointed to the continuing rise in expenses, a 'constant theme' of his statements over the previous three years, which had not slackened. In fact it had intensified. Rates, taxes, wages – there was not a heading in the expense account which did not show an

154

increase. As a result, the fight for higher turnover and increased margins became fiercer, and the need to make the best use of assets more urgent. More concentrated efforts had to be made to maximize the use of the enormous buying power of the organization, which – from its small beginnings at 44 Wigmore Street, a little shop with perhaps 20 feet of frontage – had now grown into the biggest department store group in the country, running over 100 stores, more than fifty smaller fashion shops, seven wholesale businesses, with two branches abroad, five manufacturing companies and employing some 27 000 people.

Three major sectors of retailing – the department stores, the Coop, and small independents – were open to the fiercest competition, and they were those deeply entrenched in town centres and often in prime sites.

The Cooperative movement was burdened with out-of-date stores, run by a tired and complacent management lulled by the false security of rationing which guaranteed its big food trade derived from the registration of 10m customer members. A burst of dynamism in the pioneering of self-service shopkeeping proved short-lived as others took up the grocery business and existing competitors built bigger help-yourself food stores, including supermarkets. Nonetheless the Coop still operated in 1966 some 238 department stores out of 760 in Britain.

No one however was more entrenched in prime sites of big cities and towns than the traditional department stores. These were sitting targets. Instead of steering away, chain stores and multiples deliberately moved alongside, inviting comparison on prices. They worked hand in hand with developers to present a combined presence alongside the big local name department stores. Whole streets, arcades and purpose-built centres bristled with the names of W. H. Smith, Marks & Spencer, British Home Stores, Woolworth, Boots, and the growing supermarket groups. No major town development could take place without their support. At first, as building controls relaxed and planning became freer as local authorities scrambled to modernize their towns, sites were plentiful and rentals low.

Sometimes, by acting in concert the developer and the big chains could even alter a town's traditional centre of gravity. More than a few department stores found shoppers crowding to another part of town, or being driven to car parks which were inconvenient for their stores. Modernizing stores took time but the chains seemed to mushroom overnight. Shopfitters could handle conversions for chains with a breathtaking speed, while refitting a large department store was a long job, often disrupting existing trade.

The impact on Debenhams staff morale was perhaps underestimated. Intensified central buying could cause many problems, yet decisions when taken had to be pressed. Most fears proved groundless as far as any loss of jobs was concerned. Yet Debenhams staff was not apparently sharing fully in the excitement that came to other growing retailers able to shatter sales records.

That there was excitement along Britain's High Streets could not be doubted. The risks being taken by Debenhams, by flying in the face of a century of decentralized buying by the stores it had taken over, were enormous.

9 'We'll stand comparison'

During my six years with the retail trade I have come to the conclusion tha[t] retailers are, in fact, just as bad, if not worse, than farmers and are always complaining about the weather.

Sir Anthony Burney,
Debenhams annual meeting, July 1977

Central buying of goods for Britain's largest group of department stores wa[s] intended to adapt their merchandising policies to fast-changing economi[c] and social conditions which had enlarged the spending power of people no[t] previously considered within the province of the medium to upper clas[s] categories of stores under its control. Nationally promoted and brande[d] products were the same, wherever they were bought, yet prices and credi[t] terms could be decisive when consumers took their decisions on where t[o] make their local purchases. In the case of chain stores, the development o[f] their own brand names created a customer loyalty. Often their goods wer[e] equivalent to standards of those sold under the manufacturer's trade names – and usually made to specification by the same manufacturer.

To meet competition, department store groups were having to 'trad[e] down' to secure a share of sales while the multiples steadily 'trade[d] upwards', breaking away from pre-war pretensions that social status coul[d] be derived from shopping at department stores. Not every customer wante[d] full-scale personal service. There was even hostility towards the mor[e] aggressive staff in some department stores where sales people were stil[l] earning commission. The process of multiples trading up broadened th[e] middle ground of retailing, producing the fiercest competition and expresse[d] by keen pricing and promotional activity.

Store buyers trained over many years, often with pre-war pedigrees, wer[e] puzzled as the weakness of their diffused buying power became exposed t[o] more competitive conditions. Competitors were adopting the most scientifi[c] methods in stock control. They undertook market research. Such researc[h] was used to monitor changes in the distribution of incomes, movements i[n] population, changes in spending habits, and the pricing policies of rivals[.] There was a tendency in the department store world for some department[s] to carry on trading in spite of obvious unprofitability. There was nervousness about reducing a reputation for standards of total service, for whic[h] stores were renowned, yet it meant space and capital were not always used to good advantage.

Many department stores had of course greatly widened their range of merchandise to increase their appeal as universal providers. They carried stocks of everything, from pins to pets. Variety combined with novelty made them multi-floored caverns through which customers could wander in temptation. Yet it meant buying resources were being spread very thinly over hundreds of suppliers, who became less interested in exclusive lines. Suppliers were tending to go to others prepared to negotiate substantial orders in return for quantity terms and fast repeat orders.

It was a sad situation, for often these were the very same suppliers for whom department stores had done so much. More than a few concerns, indeed, had grown through the encouragement of some store buyer who had seen the original potential of their products. Within department after department could be found examples of excessive ranges which might be simplified by adopting fewer sizes and rationalization of price ranges. Another weakness was the fact that, as the quality of buyers declined, one department's service might be at odds with another. This was particularly the case in some fashions, where a buyer might be supplying a consistent flow of garments while accessories and other things fell below what was required as the customer moved from one department to another.

Shops within shops were often set up by leasing out space to specialists. Not all were consistent with the master store's trading 'image' and by definition the development of shops within stores was intended to make use of others' skills. Those customers who experienced this development began to feel that they might just as well go to other specialist shops outside. Even the best leased shops within department stores raised confusion in customers' minds, especially when they were offered stock for which alternatives existed elsewhere within the master store.

Multiples were succeeding because they were not just using their buying power, but also because they integrated the retailing and wholesaling function in distribution. Branch managers were loyal to headquarters, presenting an impression of uniformity and style which could be reflected in national promotion. Shoppers in a chain store in Rochdale felt they had the same opportunities as in London or some other big city. Multiples were able to analyse sales results quickly to collaborate with suppliers in marketing schemes, or limited sales tests of some garment or household appliance which might be offered in all stores.

The war years had cleft retailing into two distinct eras. Post-war years brought millions of married women into employment whether working part or full-time. Nearly 2½m marriages took place between 1939 and 1945. The population bought cars, switched from cinemas to television sets and record players for entertainment. They bought refrigerators in which to store convenience foods and demanded a host of new packaged items for the pantry. They opened bank accounts, and expected credit to enlarge their spending power. Shopping had to take account of their increasing use of cars. Mail order trading grew sharply, especially among customers in rural areas. Frozen foods, detergent washing powders, and transistorized radio were typical

post-war products, and the commercial television service was increasingl
used by manufacturers and big shopkeepers as a powerful new means o
promoting their goods or sales events.

Young middle income groups articulated demands for more consume
protection and supported development of an organized consumer move
ment. Supermarkets grew bigger and better, and new discounters added t
the pressures of price competition. Holidays with pay became universal and
in retailing, shop hours were controlled by authorities. Competition fo
trained sales people grew while, to many youngsters, a career in the retai
trade was no longer considered quite so attractive.

One of the most fundamental trends was the erosion of resale pric
maintenance. Many suppliers of nationally branded goods were fighting
rearguard action. In general, modern shopkeepers, who once supported th
idea of collectively or individually enforced conditions of sale, disliked an
dictation from suppliers. Debenhams was strongly opposed to the practice o
suppliers attempting to fix shop prices and the organization decided not t
hesitate in cutting selected prices in order to match particular competition
Debenhams' early policy for the central buying of electrical goods was a
example of aggressiveness suited to the times.

Not until January 1965, when a Government order under the *Resale Price*
Act 1964 banned price fixing for all goods not registered for court investiga
tion, was RPM nailed into an official coffin. Debenhams had its share o
troubles. Kayser Bondor, for example, always added a cautionary note to it
invoices ('The acceptance of this invoice is an undertaking that the good
entered therein will be offered for sale at prices specified upon the company'
price list.') The struggle by some suppliers to keep price maintenance coin
cided with the introduction by Debenhams of central buying, and it coul
not have been an easy time for the stores, which were faced with legal action
and blockaded supplies of goods if they infringed conditions of sale previ
ously permitted under the terms of the *Restrictive Trades Practices Act* 1956

However, department stores such as Debenhams and the John Lewis Part
nership were not going to let supermarkets claim all the credit with consum
ers for resisting attempts by suppliers to enforce standard minimum prices
Supermarket operators broke down food price maintenance and, alway
anxious for publicity, soon moved on to dry goods, which they did not sel
in great quantity but, by obtaining supplies and conducting hit-and-run pric
cuts, created an impression of championing the consumer cause. During th
sixties, Britain's retail trade competed hard and vigorously, demonstratin
the virtues of free enterprise while raising its efficiency.

There was a new boldness among shopkeepers of all shapes and sizes
Even small independent store owners began to band together into buyin
groups. The erosion of price maintenance, coinciding with the release of
pent-up demand for a better standard of living, was a surging force fo
change from which neither Debenhams nor any other department stor
operators could escape.

Just how department stores fared, as a sector, before their reorganizatio
can be seen from the Census of Distribution, monitoring changes betwee
1961 and 1967. In this time, seven out of every 100 shops closed but retai

trade rose 26 per cent, reflecting a trend to larger units, mainly in the food sector. Household goods stores pushed up sales by nearly 35 per cent, well above the average, but department stores were only able to reach a shade under 20 per cent.

Numbers employed in department stores, which remained labour intensive, fell from 164 000 to 157 000. Turnover per person between 1961 and 1966 rose 25 per cent from £3321 to £4162 whereas that for cooperatives advanced 23 per cent from £5200 to £6416 without the same overheads and that for multiples 32 per cent from £4682 to £6173.

Britain was served in 1961 by 784 department stores with combined sales of £546m. In 1966 there were twenty-four fewer stores and turnover was £653m. Sales of household goods shops, clothing and footwear and other non-food retailers boomed. Multiple shopkeepers pushed up annual trade by a mighty £1 300 000 000.

Redevelopment and closures by Debenhams were intended to safeguard trade and, by central buying, use the reorganized stores for a rising volume of trade compensating for lower margins.

To organize bulk buying on the scale required for such a large enterprise was no mean task, particularly in a group which had built itself up on a large degree of local initiative. The group had for some years centrally bought some basic lines to compete with the multiples, but these goods, made to its own specification and design, were only sold in selected stores described officially as 'catering for the mass media'. There had been nearly ten years of prevarication, even though central buying began in 1957 by establishing Debenhams' footwear division which by 1966 supplied over 120 shoe departments. In 1960 Debenhams Electrical and Radio Distribution was formed, and fairly rapid progress was now being made, with the sole distribution rights for Sony television and radio receivers, and there was later an agency for Bang & Olufsen goods.

The group had also enlarged the list of products offered under its own brand names. Sale of food within the organization had increased enormously in the past decade. Some sixty-four traditional restaurants and fifteen self-service restaurants were in operation while seventeen food departments and eight self-service food halls had been established. The trend was to purchase food in bulk as far as possible to meet the challenge of a very competitive market. The chain of Cresta Fashion shops had grown by 1966 to fifty-one retail outlets.

In 1966, John Bedford announced his board's decision to adopt central buying in all stores. He commented: 'This is probably the most revolutionary decision that Debenhams have had to make, but we are convinced that in the changed circumstances it is the right decision. It confronts the directors and the management teams with a tremendous challenge.'

Bedford marshalled his resources. Properties had been revalued in the spring of 1965 and were worth approximately £90m. During the past ten years, the pattern of retail distribution had been rapidly changing, as he explained:

We have seen the growth of the chain store operation, the development of the speciality shops, discount stores, and out-of-town shopping. To this is added the

tremendous growth of the mail order business. Department stores, if they are t
survive against this intensified competition, will need to change with the change
circumstances.

Central buying would become essential. More departments were to be lai
out on a pre-selection basis – the customer would virtually serve herself, an
an increasing number of departments were to go over to complete sel
service. With the traffic congestion in major cities, the group would loo
afresh at the prospect of 'out-of-town' developments, already commonplac
in America.

Dealing with the theme that the abandonment of price maintenance, th
growth of mail order business, the establishment of discount houses, and th
increase in multiple shops would have a serious effect on the future c
department stores, Bedford recorded that fifteen years before, this view ha
been expressed in the United States where they were subject to far mor
competition. However, after an initial setback, the US stores had not onl
weathered the storm but they were playing an increasingly important part i
retail distribution.

In Britain the development of new towns had proved that, without
department store, a shopping area lacked the focal point which the public no
only appreciated but needed to make shopping a pleasure. 'I am convince
that if department stores face the challenge of the future with initiative an
enterprise, they will emerge after the initial setback stronger than eve
before,' he declared.

These words of John Bedford, in 1966, indicated a setback ahead. Hi
prophesy was fulfilled but he vacated the chairman's seat before the change
authorized in his time could be judged as appropriate. Openings and closure
(including Woollands in Knightsbridge) continued as the going becam
rougher and the switch to central buying caused inevitable internal turmoil

Below: *Woollands millinery
advertisement from between the
wars* The Illustrated London
News Picture Library

Below right: *An early Woollands trade card*

Antony Burney

Some very hard decisions had to be taken. Some of the provincial stores of Marshall & Snelgrove were grossly overstocked with overvalued and unsaleable goods. A two-year struggle to put things right ended in closures and write-downs. The imposition of selective employment tax took up valuable management time during a critical period. Annual group profits after tax fell between 1966 and 1968. Early in 1969 John Bedford said he had no desire to make excuses for results which were frankly disappointing. Press comment was sharp and hints of a take-over bid disturbed confidence.

Intensive reorganization was matched by boardroom changes with a number of retirements overshadowed by the decision in 1970 of John Bedford to surrender management control to a new deputy chairman and chief executive, A. J. Smith, an experienced regional director recruited to the main board a year before. Executive structure was then shaken up by the appointment of new regional controllers and three managing directors. Amid the changes, men arrived from outside the organization – Ken Bishop came from a tobacco company as a director dealing with financial affairs, and Sir Anthony Burney who joined the board on a part-time basis in October 1970.

Burney's arrival was intriguing. It seemed that Bedford was preparing for his succession, though Debenhams had never had an outsider as its chairman. City confidence had to be improved and Burney, an accountant with a distinguished record, came into the boardroom with other directorships to his name, including the mighty Commercial Union Assurance Company, International Computers (Holdings) and Stone Platt Industries. Internal speculation was well founded and John Bedford, who retired in April 1971, made way for Sir Anthony to move in February 1971 into the chairman's office at 1 Welbeck Street.

The new Rugby and Cambridge educated chairman was regarded with apprehension. He was a very different character from Bedford. A good humoured and dominant man, his eyes would crinkle, as he shook hands firmly with the executives he had to galvanize and to the staff needing reassurance. In broad lapelled suits and broad striped shirts, he exuded confidence. He knew the wider world of finance as a partner in Binder, Hamlyn & Co. A colonel in war, he understood the nature of change since 1945 and had seen its impact when he was director of reorganization for the Cotton Board between 1959 and 1960. He had contacts in Whitehall which had invited him to serve in the mid-sixties on the Shipbuilding Inquiry Committee. Above all he was an expert on management accounting.

Yet what was important was his level of understanding of the nature of social change and the role Debenhams had to find in modern retailing. Burney was a modern, understanding man whose interests included the Charities' Aid Fund, membership of the executive committee of the National Council of Social Service, photography and gardening. His interest in people and their problems belied the reputation of accountants for cold calculation and preferences for figures. Nonetheless many charts and statistics were prepared under his direction to establish the magnitude of Debenhams' problems.

Profits after tax had slumped from £4.3m in 1968 to £3.7m in 1969 and the following year, 1970, they fell to under £3.3m. This alarming trend was reversed in Burney's first year, for in 1971 the profits recovered sharply to £4.8m.

The New Year sales came and went. Then followed not so much a crisis but one of those unexpected emergencies which in business marks one year out from many others. Historians call them pendulum years, and the crucial event came in a Leap Year when February had five days to run.

24 February 1972 was not to be just another day as staff reported for work throughout the Debenhams organization. There was a feeling of anarchy touching everyone. Less than twenty-four hours before, five women and a Padre, had died in the bombing by Irish terrorists of the 16th Parachute Brigade's mess at Aldershot and precautions were being taken in stores. Britain was in the grip of a three-day working week for manufacturing and severe restrictions on lighting and heating, prompted by a national strike of coal miners. The morning papers had been full of the Prime Minister's warnings that the Government would stand firm on pay deals.

For their part, Debenhams executives sipped their quick cups of coffee and glanced over copies of the *Financial Times*, which was carrying a major article on out-of-town shopping centres. In the small print of stock market prices, sharp rises were being recorded for both Debenhams and United Drapery Stores. Before the day was over, Debenhams' share price soared from 68p to 348p.

At the London headquarters, executives spent the morning on telephones and shifting paper, some going into committee rooms for working conferences. Lunchtime was much as usual – banter and some talk about Edward Heath's political problems. The afternoon began in the usual frenzy of men preoccupied with pressing problems as a smartly dressed Justice of the Peace presented himself at reception and asked for an interview at the highest level.

The caller was Bernard Lyons, who had spent some time preparing for this moment. Lyons was the chairman of the United Drapery Stores combine, owner of more than 1,200 shops and stores. He was ushered upstairs and, after a preliminary encounter with A. J. Smith, chief executive, was hurriedly escorted to see Debenhams' chairman. The grapevine of the executive suite buzzed as Lyons politely greeted Burney and slapped down a letter on the chairman's desk.

Such was the beginning, for Debenhams at least, of a take-over bid worth £114 000 000. Mr Lyons explained his view that an amalgamation would bring together two complementary businesses, but he touched a nerve when he told Sir Anthony that UDS could do much to make Debenhams more prosperous for the benefit of both groups' shareholders. Sir Anthony gave Lyons a courteous but brief hearing, letting him use the telephone to call Hill Samuel. The letter was a document outlining the proposal which had been a month in preparation by UDS's financial advisers, Hill Samuel, the merchant bankers.

When Lyons was escorted from the premises, Burney sat for a few moments, collecting his thoughts. Soon he was on the telephone to Morgan Grenfell and later drove to the City, to take counsel. Later as news agency machines in Fleet Street tapped out the first messages in advance of fuller statements from UDS, specialist writers thumbed through files on the two groups. Unlike Bedford before him, Burney understood the importance of newspapers, which would be read by shareholders. By the evening, reporters were put through on the telephone, and Burney made Debenhams' position crystal clear. 'Totally inadequate,' he barked decisively, a phrase that bought time but let the world know his position.

Meetings were set up with Morgan Grenfell and Kleinwort Benson the next day to discuss in some detail a defence against Lyons's ambitions to create the world's largest departmental store group. The problem was that UDS offered performance, whereas Debenhams promised performance in terms of returns to shareholders. It was not easy to work out a strategy to repel the invader. Yet there was one factor favouring Debenhams – its trading results had started to improve and a property revaluation, of some importance in destroying the UDS share valuation, was in hand. Burney knew about take-over struggles and had indeed been deeply involved in the dramatic fight between ICI and Courtaulds.

A small 'war room' was created and Burney brought in Charles Ball from Kleinworts and a public relations expert, John Addey, to plan the Debenhams strategy.

It is difficult for those not close to such events to understand the feelings of the people on the receiving end of such a colossal bid. Managers can be demoralized, even start arguing among themselves. There is always an emotive factor since people's livelihoods and careers are suddenly threatened. The logic of a merger and the facts and figures pushed out from rival camps are, nonetheless, important to shareholders and Government, with the latter taking an increasing interest in merger deals.

Burney's initial decision to stand and fight, taken without hesitation, was extremely important to those around him. Once it was seen the chairman had the situation under firm control, executives were encouraged to get on with running the business while the 'war room' handled the take-over battle.

On paper, UDS looked a formidable adversary. From ownership of five department stores in 1927, when it was incorporated, UDS was a multi-faceted group spanning mail order, menswear, twenty-one department stores, and manufacturing. It owned Allders of Croydon, Arding & Hobbs of London, Whiteleys of Bayswater, Swears & Wells, Shinners of Sutton, ran the much praised Richard chain of 132 fashion shops ('Such Clever Clothes'), and operated the John Myers mail order concern. Other interests included over 650 menswear stores trading as John Collier ('The Window to Watch'), Alexandre and Claud Alexander. Turnover was more than £166m.

Those within Debenhams with long memories recalled the ill-fated moves of their past management to beat Swears & Wells for the return of Cavendish House in Cheltenham. In more recent times, there had been Bedford's honourable refusal to buy UDS shares in Harrods when it pulled out of its struggle with Debenhams and the House of Fraser for control of the Knightsbridge-based group. Others looked up UDS's efforts to buy Montague Burton, which in 1967 had foundered on the rocks of an adverse Monopolies Commission report.

An early move was to advise shareholders not to take any action when they received the formal offer documents sent out to shareholders under the City's rules for take-overs and mergers. UDS had quietly bought up a block of 235 000 shares between 14 January and 18 February 1972 – six days before Lyons's arrival without prior appointment at Debenhams' headquarters. Whitehall was unconcerned and announced it would not send the contested merger to the Monopolies Commission.

Burney now decided to turn Debenhams' apparent disadvantage in trading under scores of local names into an opportunity for combining staff feeling by a decision to identify stores more closely with his organization. All executives and staff received posters, car stickers, lapel badges and leaflets. 'Keep Debenhams Independent' and 'We Are a Debenhams Store' were typical messages to customers, many of them including small shareholders. Thousands of customers were suddenly made aware that their favourite Plummers, Bobbys, Jones, Curls, and Pauldens stores – to name just a few – were actually owned by Debenhams and somehow threatened by an alien ownership. Store directors were encouraged by Sir Anthony to use their goodwill with local newspapers to focus attention outside London on the take-over struggle.

The City was impressed at Debenhams' refusal to show any weakness and, indeed, the way in which Debenhams was beginning to take the offensive spoke a lot for the determination of the new chairman as well as his confidence after the weary years of reorganization and as yet unfulfilled promises of better trading results. Shareholders received records and those without players were invited to stores, where managers kept record players handy so they might hear a message from the chairman. If that was a novelty to veteran observers of take-over battles, more important was a letter to shareholders accompanying results for the year to the end of January 1972.

Debenhams' campaign to remain independent
Above: *Lapel Badge*
Right: *Record sleeve*
Far right: *Letter to shareholders*

Debenhams Limited

1 Welbeck Street London W1A 1DF
Telegrams: Debenham London W1
Telephone: 01-580 4444 Telex: 27124

Dear Shareholder,

Inside this sleeve is a record which contains a personal message from me to you.

If you do not have a record player yourself any Debenhams store will be delighted to play it for you.

This message emphasises how important it is that you should NOT SIGN any document sent to you by UDS

Yours sincerely,

Anthony Burney

The Directors of Debenhams have taken all reasonable care to ensure that the facts and opinions expressed herein and in the enclosed record are fair and accurate and they jointly and severally accept responsibility for such facts and opinions.

**LETTER FROM
DEBENHAMS LIMITED
ADVISING REJECTION
OF THE OFFER
MADE BY
UNITED DRAPERY STORES**

DEBENHAMS BELONGS TO YOU

**THEREFORE
DO NOT SIGN
ANY DOCUMENTS
SENT TO YOU BY UDS**

Pre-tax profits were up nearly £1.4m and, more pertinent, dividends were lifted, an encouragement to hang on.

In a perceptive comment, *The Times* said: 'Although not spectacular, pre-tax profits for the year to end January from Debenhams may be enough to hold off UDS.' With property revaluation and benefits of store rationalization to come, shareholders 'should sit tight'.

First sign of a weakening by UDS came on 13 April 1972, when the UDS board increased their offer for Debenhams by £19m to £132m, a package of shares, alternative cash payments, and convertible stock by now familiar to Debenhams board. Burney said the price was not in the right ball park. Shareholders should not be asked to give two-thirds of their growth potential in exchange for paper in a company which he thought was 'ex-growth'. The new offer, he said scathingly, was a 'face saver'.

The experienced Burney noted that a deadline on the UDS offer could not be extended without a new round of City underwriting. The fact that the UDS price was now above the Debenhams market price did not worry him, for it would keep out counter bidders, such as Sir Charles Clore's Sears Holdings, which had been rumoured to be showing more than a passing interest. For Lyons, the problem was to break down Debenhams' public barricades. He delivered a massive broadside in the shape of a promise to double Debenhams' profits to around £15m, a year before tax under UDS control.

Lyons openly criticised Debenhams' top management. Peering benevolently over his half-moon glasses, the grey-haired Lyons on 17 April met the press, promising a better return on sales through the merged group, which he would call United Debenhams Stores. Harvey Nichols' store in Knightsbridge would remain separate and distinctive, but he was non-committal about Debenham & Freebody in Wigmore Street, already scheduled for redevelopment. In reply, Burney, carefully writing to shareholders, claimed great trading success from an interest free credit sales drive and promised to write again. He told the newspapers Debenhams would not provide any profit forecast.

There was now a sharper tone to Burney's rejection of the improved offer. Indeed, there was open anger when it was discovered that UDS was carrying out market research among the 46 000 shareholders, canvassing opinion on the Debenhams record. Relationships with UDS had already been soured by a brightly produced document circulated by Lyons's advisers which compared some individual stores in each group, such as Allders and Kennards in Croydon, and Richard Shops against Cresta Silks. The brochure carried the message, 'We'll Stand Comparison.' Out went new lapel badges from Debenhams, declaring, 'Debenhams Will Be Better On Their Own.'

The structure of Debenhams shareholdings was an important consideration. Since institutions only commanded 30 per cent, it was vital to maintain the support of small shareholders. This was part of the reason why UDS was striking at the grass roots support by sending round researchers, and explained the extraordinary sight of floorwalkers and sales assistants displaying anti-UDS badges. Comparisons about sales per square foot of store space flew like bullets, and Burney prepared to play two trump cards as time ran out on the deadline for acceptance of the UDS offer by shareholders. On 27 April, he played the first – a property redevelopment scheme promising a big boost to income from rentals and, before he could put down the second (a profits forecast for £10.5m in 1972), on 3 May UDS conceded defeat. Its offer had lapsed through insufficient acceptances.

Walking down a corridor, one senior executive, David Pope, now controller of selling, heard a commotion and then met the chief executive, A. J. Smith, hands aloft in triumph. 'We've won – we've won,' shouted Smith. 'They've dropped the bid.' That night a flock of jubilant Debenhams managers went a Retail Distributors Association dinner, and for some the celebrations continued into the early hours at Smith's London flat. There were sore heads and red eyes the next morning. The chairman, who had not been tempted to make any wild profits forecast during the fight, now ordered one to be published. The executives would not be allowed to forget that Debenhams, under threat, had become unified as never before and that they must act decisively to obtain greater efficiency.

Debenhams' shareholders received a swift letter from Burney, disclosing the profits forecast as evidence of good faith and encouragement. He wrote: 'I am confident that you will not regret your decision to keep your shares.'

The record speaks for itself. In 1972, trading profits before interest reached nearly £10.7m, and within four years they were doubled at almost £22m. These were years now called by Debenhams as 'Burney's Dash For Growth'. The now blooded and ebullient accountant ordered faster redevelopment and more ruthless closures. The Bedford years, whose painful but necessary reforms owed much to the former chairman, were clearly over. Debenhams had a new status in City circles and the take-over fight had finally dispelled any lingering impression that the group was run by tired people out of tune with their times.

Burney's battle had welded top level staff into a unity of purpose which would be retained, channelling enthusiasm for his leadership into a steady drive to broaden the base of the business. Before that exciting year was over, and, indeed by that summer, the chairman had done something about the failure to embrace the grocery trade. At the time of the covetous approach from UDS, Burney had been talking to Leslie Cater, chairman of Cater Brothers, which had long run supermarkets in southern England.

Kennedy Cater

Negotiations on a possible association between Debenhams and Caters had to be suspended during the take-over fight and, in the interim, there was tragedy for the supermarkets group, for Leslie Cater was killed in an air crash in France. His cousin Mr Kennedy Cater took up the negotiations and by the August of 1972 Debenhams had bought the entire share capital for £8·4m.

Burney considered that, with its large property portfolio, Debenhams now had a strong asset base from which to expand. At the same time, resources had to be freed by overhauling the traditional department store operations. Over 333 000 'option account' credit cards were issued to replace existing credit facilities available to customers, and a major review of all stores began. Within a year, some twenty-one small stores were closed, or sold to others. It looked like savagery, but valuable property resources were being released into Debenhams' balance sheets. Stores vanished one after the other as the branches were pruned.

Closures and sales included Plummer shops at Andover, Boscombe, Bournemouth, Folkestone, Southend, and Yeovil. Bobbys' name disappeared from Margate and Cliftonville. Greys branches at Leamington, Rugby, Solihull, Stourbridge and Worcester went. The axe fell on one after another. Williams & Hopkins at Bournemouth, Barrance & Ford at Brighton, Gammans at Woking, Robinsons at Darlington, Peal in London, Tuttles at Lowestoft, Affleck & Brown at Manchester, Farmers of Nottingham, Jones at Kingswood, Bristol, and the Bon Marché branch at Poole.

This drastic programme was parallelled by a programme of acquisitions which included the take-over in June 1973 of H & M Rayne, a chain of high fashion footwear shops with interests in the United States and France. Within the month, Debenhams made an even more ambitious purchase – the 125 footwear stores trading under the Lotus name. At the same time, an investment was made in the Hardy Amies design consultancy business associated with the Hepworths tailoring group. J & S Bickley, a clothing manufacturer, was added to the list by October.

Just before the start of Christmas trading in 1973, the deputy chairman and chief executive resigned. The chairman set up a small executive committee, then a new chief executive was found from outside. He was Bob Thornton, who, when he came in during 1974, rapidly established his authority, brooking little argument as decisions streamed out. Debenhams seemed to be in turmoil but Thornton, made deputy chairman the following year, set a series

Hardy Amies, Saville Row

Hardy Amies Collections
Left to right: *1972   1973
1973/4   1974*   International
Wool Secretariat Photograph

of objectives for lowering expenses and pushing forward the reorganization
of department stores, now headed by a tough main board director, Tony
Barnsley. Sale and leaseback deals on freehold premises, including the headquarters in Welbeck Street, London, provided badly needed funds to pay for
all the reforms.

A small business, Derek Gardner, specialists in photographic equipment,
was bought in 1973.

Meanwhile work had started on a comprehensive redevelopment of the
Harvey Nichols store in Knightsbridge. There were numerous problems
during this period, 1973-76. A venture in audio equipment involving
Amerex proved a disaster. The Cresta business was remodelled with the help
of the renowned Miss Winifred Sainer, sister of Sir Charles Clore's deputy
chairman Leonard Sainer and founder of the Miss Selfridge fashion bou-
tiques. Turnover began to nudge up towards £300 000 000. There was a flow
of boardroom changes as well as new deals, including the purchase of the
Hamleys toy business (1976), Greens Camera Shops & Leisure Centres
(1976), and the historic Browns department store at Chester (1976).

And still the acquisitions continued. To the list was added, in 1976, the
Cavendish Medical Centre and, in 1977, New Dimension Furniture. At the
time of writing, money was being raised under a deal to release the Scan
superstore at Walkden, Manchester, and another superstore at Nottingham
to Tesco, which also agreed to buy the historic Busby store at Bradford.

Institutions such as pension funds and insurance companies queued to join
the share registers, supporting the massive changes introduced by Burney
since 1971. The results speak for themselves. In 1970 annual net profit before
tax was just over £5m, but by 1977 the profit was well over £18m.

It is still a too recent and too turbulent period upon which to pronounce a
view, but there can be no doubt that the balance sheets of Debenhams say
something about the changes which have been wrought. No more difficult a

decision, however, could there have been than to adopt nationally the Debenhams name for the 70 surviving department stores, including the world famous Marshall & Snelgrove in Oxford Street.

The modern uniform Debenhams chain was a not smooth progression. Certainly an untidy history stood in the way of numerous bands of managers, as they reached their decisions. Business was conducted in an exciting round of internal argument, at times friendly, occasionally acrimonious. Management is not a bland process, rather a fascinating clash between strategists with the aim of meeting competition from without. They will differ, even suffer. People rise and fall, serving their time according to their best abilities.

A thought has to be spared for those inevitable casualties within any enterprise. There are lessons to be learned, however, from the past. Frederick Scott Oliver wrote:

No one who has ever engaged in business is unfamiliar with the quandary that presents itself when the occupant of some important position is discovered to be unfit for his job. It is in essence the same quandary whether he be a silk buyer, or a credit clerk, or the superintendent of a factory, or a managing director, or a highly placed civil servant, or a general in the field, or a Cabinet minister.

A very wide freedom of choice has this disadvantage, that the chooser is apt to pick the men who will be the easiest to work with; and these are not necessarily the men who will do their work best.

Debenhams made and admits to many mistakes over its 200 years in history, yet it survived because there was always replacement and displacement of people, and trading was based on a durable concept of excellence in their ideas for storekeeping. The epoch of scientific management may have arrived, but the heart which beats strongly within Debenhams is still the department store, changing in the presentation of its services, but always relevant.

169

10 *Blurring boundaries*

The future comes after the past.
Otherwise it couldn't be the future ...

Alan Bennett, *Twenty Years On*

Modern department stores have a long pedigree. They have been as grandly
designed or purposefully-run as their owners, at each stage of their history
wanted them to be. Each developed an ambience and style still defended by
their ageing devotees when the stores are threatened by some supposed
foreign management bent on change or even demolition.

Yet what is so striking about Britain's department stores, given their long
history, has been the willingness of managements to anticipate social trends
rebuilding or redesigning shop interiors and sales floors. Accusations that
any changes or closures represent acts of architectural vandalism and dimin-
ish our High Street heritage may continue to grow, even among generations
of shoppers whose interest in conservation can be stimulated without experience of past standards in trading. But such buildings have no other purpose
than to serve the community, which needs stores appropriate to their practical requirements. Traders are not museum-keepers, though they are sometimes sentimental.

Browns of Chester or Harvey Nichols and Harrods in London's
Knightsbridge survive because they justify their existence on the basis of a
stated purpose – to sell goods at a profit. It is for the customers to decide the
question of survival by the prices they are prepared to pay, and the value of
any store reflected in its stock and its service may be measured by prices and
turnover. Any management which neglects the discipline of profit lessens
the chances of survival, for expenses are never stable in running any business. A fine old store where madam is attended by her favourite sales assistant until a satisfactory purchase may or may not be made cannot be sustained unless madam will pay a sufficient price to cover the cost – and there
are not enough people with incomes to nourish such service.

Many fine stores have been lost in the past century through complacent
managements which presumed their manners and methods were divinely
inspired and inviolate from the competition of newcomers, ranging from the
earliest chain stores to the well-organized supermarket operators and aggressive multiple shopkeepers. What such managements confused was the durability of the concept of departmentalized trading under one roof with its

vulnerability when not properly applied to prevailing consumer requirements.

Department stores were slow to appreciate the importance of their heritage in terms of the 'written down' values of their occupancy of prime town centre sites. Others thought it unnecessary to realize capital from deals and revaluation when all around them was evidence of a property boom. One view of the times was that of a typical developer, Edward Erdman, engaged in persuading retailers to see opportunities for modernization with the help of property experts. During the post-war boom, which was not caused entirely by blind speculation, he set down the following thoughts on the transformation:

The old traditional department store, with its frock-coated manager to direct customers to respective departments, has given way to the modern department store, with its direction indicators, fast-moving escalators, and merchandise usually arranged for self-service. The genial local grocer of the past with a ready dialogue on weather conditions has given place to the extensive self-service supermarket where you take a trolley, serve yourself and pay at the turnstile. The crowded market street lined with stalls, with shoppers pushing shoulder to shoulder in complete discomfort but enjoying the atmosphere created by the quips of the street traders and the quest for bargains, is fast being displaced by the modern covered market.

The unplanned, ever extending, straggling narrow High Street of the past with no focal point, shoppers over-flowing the pavements into the road, which is often also the main traffic artery filled with buses, delivery vans serving the shops and private cars unable to park, is gradually being transformed. Progressive measures are being taken to cure the traffic problem: traffic diversions, 'One Way Only', parking meters; subsequently some High Streets have become fully pedestrianized by all traffic being siphoned off round a ring road.

Traffic hazards, more motorists, the need for extra car parking, and rear servicing for shops combined with the price of land in the busiest part of the High Street – much of which was already owned by leading retailers – encouraged shopping developers to build new centres in depth with frontage to the High Street, but utilizing less expensive back land, known as shopping precincts. Many of these have been successful in areas which were not already over-shopped, and where these were grafted skilfully onto the main shopping centre with continuity of shopping flow and with one of the large stores as a shopping generator. An essential ingredient is an exit into another thoroughfare and good car parking.

Those who became custodians of stores founded on excellence of service in splendid surroundings were foolish to rest on traditions alone. Too many were distracted by the glorious past from adapting their business to the future. This is not to say that a magnificent store with great traditions cannot survive. Many did. The survivors never lost sight of the need to maintain profitability. Fine stores and traditions were preserved when they made good commercial sense and, if costs went wrong, others moved in to dictate the necessary changes, as brash or subtle as their business judgement indicated.

Each owner, or parent group, will freely acknowledge that no customers owe them a living and no store can owe another a living if competition is to flourish in the universal interest of consumers. In the Soviet Union, GUM would not survive long in spite of magnificent premises if consumers were to be offered western choice and competitive merchandising. Great name such as Harrods, Bentalls, Liberty's, Beattie, Bourne & Hollingsworth, Selfridges survive today because customers are willing to pay their prices, high and low, and like their modern services, including choice of stock. They are increasingly dependent on generations of shoppers who cannot recall retailing in by-gone times and to whom the supermarket or functional chain store seem natural.

And yet there lingers in the mind a feeling that department stores are really something special. Even those linoleum-floored barns with creaking lifts and antiquated overhead cash-to-receipt desk mechanisms may be remembered or described to the young with nostalgia, by those who forget the dust, flies and articles of dubious quality and little if any packaging. In the epoch of guarantees, exchange, money back, and burgeoning legislation – applying to both retailers and suppliers – this nostalgia can be misleading. Competitors of department stores, in spite of their power and size, still appear rootless as they continue to invade every High Street and available central site.

Could it be that theirs is a restless search for the identity which department stores still enjoy and which evokes the nostalgia? The bland uniformity of multiples, supermarkets, and chains admittedly pushes up profits and turnover, but it is nonetheless evident that each has begun to invade the other's trade.

The successful combines and chains tend to crowd together, and even the first out-of-town developments depend on the property promoters attracting the big name retailers to share together the rented space and to reduce the risks from isolated trading. New arcades and traffic-free shopping precincts, a feature of many post-war developments which have been as profound in their impact on high street architecture as Victorian building, are notable for the concentration of the principal combatants in what is always called the High Street war. The multiplicity of names, perhaps, gives to such developments the identity which each seeks. They may not share the same entrance, just the central footways and covered thoroughfares, but the herding together suggests the department store concept in another form.

A department store group such as Debenhams embraces the trends in another way by inviting into its substantial premises more and more companies (some of which it owns) to operate as shops within a store, exploiting the concept of one-stop shopping developed over 200 years by using the skills of others alongside its own services, including much centrally bought stock and easy credit.

There is truth in the phrase that traditions die hard, according to Tony Wilson, sales director of Debenhams and the man who reorganized the old Marshall & Snelgrove store in Oxford Street:

Everyone seemed to think that if you had a store that was part of a community, it must necessarily trade under its old name, otherwise customers would be lost. After all, the name of a store is only made up of the ingredients of staff, merchandise, and service. An old name guarantees nothing in itself. We refused to play King Canute. There is a mass maelstrom of the public passing the stores in the crush of a modern High Street. To aim at specific socio-economic groups you were really saying to all those people: 'You can come in, but you cannot. Perhaps you might, but not you

Above: *Tony Wilson*

Above right: *The new Marshall & Snelgrove store*

madam, until you are earning more or have a better status.'

This is nonsense. We have to take into account all the changes in disposable income and the fact that working families with a rented home, for example, deserve our attention. Sometimes they will have more in terms of disposable income than say a rising executive burdened with a mortgage and kiddies on private education. So we say, this is the range of merchandise and anyone is welcome to come in and buy, irrespective of class, colour, and creed. We are here to serve you all.

To my mind, a department store exists for a variety of reasons. People can escape from the other stores. They come to browse, to wander, to be motivated, initiated, and, yes, seduced into desiring our merchandise. It is no use longing for the past. Service is no longer a carpet on the floor, a chair, and an assistant for each customer – that would require doubling prices. People want value for their money, and they do not have the time for service at a funereal pace.

However, when people walk into our stores we want them to sense something, perhaps pleasure, or fun, in shopping. Ambience is partly about how people feel. You can sense a difference, for example, when you walk into some houses.

Department stores are the sheet anchors of High Streets and shopping malls. Our task is to look ahead five, ten, fifteen years, and beyond, and to ask ourselves how do we get there?

Groups like Debenhams, which owned many originally autonomous stores, have regained their confidence with the application of new capital and managements which came to terms with the problems of size. In the case of Debenhams, confidence in itself was regained once its management realized that it had never lost the true identity of the business. While it was true there were many separate trading houses with many different names rooted in neighbourhood shopkeeping, the business never began to realize the full potential until someone somewhere saw the advantages of using the most historic single family name in British retail history.

Perhaps this was recognized many years ago but not acted upon. But the modern management has had the capacity to undertake what appears to be the unpleasant task of putting up the real name of the owner of the stores. Debenhams is a family of stores, with great grandfathers, grandfathers,

173

fathers and lusty new infants of shops. Of course, it is an irony of the group's history that it has a diffused share ownership and two of the most important men among the custodians of this old retailing combine are outsiders.

Sir Anthony Burney, the chairman, and the chief executive and deputy chairman, Bob Thornton, have imposed authority in both direction and management of what was becoming a rambling empire. They have confounded critics, who have included the author, by producing trading results of some consequence. The 1970s, which saw their arrival, have been nonetheless a painful and exacting, if exciting, period, not without frequent internal argument and even clashes of brute personality among executives pressing their ideas.

The departmental stores sector of retailing is full of theorists, self-confessed hard school practitioners believing in hunch and instinct, gentle souls from the past, and young men seeing in its businesses chances to train in every aspect of trading. Personalities are known across the boundaries of store groups, exchanging banter at the kind of trade dinners and functions which businessmen like to suffer gladly. One such man is Debenhams' chief of department stores, Anthony Barnsley, a blunt, long serving Debenhams director with a history of experience in the multiple shops and chain stores as well as department stores, whose relentless insistence on using ground floors to the fullest advantage and his advocacy of new layouts when rebuilding or opening new stores has been invigorating.

He says with no hint of hesitation:

Anthony Barnsley

> The department store can cope with the modern customer if those who run it are confident and carry the staff with them. We have to be salesmen at every point and must use our huge selling space in the coordinated way of these times. Our move to central buying over 10 years or so was slow and gradual, and picked off the easiest items such as linens and finished with the hardest, ladies fashions. Okay, our slowness might be criticized, but central buying does not meet every store's needs and the use of shops-within-shops offers a selection of merchandise and highly specialist selling skills, whether for Windsmoor fashions, Wedgwood china and glass, or even antiques. The one rule is that everything must pay its way.

Bob Thornton

From behind a glass-topped desk, Bob Thornton, chief executive, commands the entire Debenhams' operation. Sales are surging towards the £500 000 000 a year mark and he sees a billion pound trade in the mid-eighties as no fanciful management target. Behind him is a doorway into the adjacent office suite of the full-time chairman, Sir Anthony Burney. The two men differ in style from those they succeeded, John Bedford and A. J. Smith, who knew Debenhams well by rising through its internal routes to the top.

Thornton's career has spanned most aspects of Marks & Spencer, where he served before moving on to a general managership and directorship at British Home Stores (which he helped to transform), and expanding United Builders Merchants. He met Burney through an introduction from Kleinworts, the City merchant banking house. The chief executive's talk is refreshingly frank and he comes quickly to his points, a sure sign of a decisive man with a strong will to obtain results from those around him, who are entitled to clear guidance. He avoids no questions and eschews

174

sentimentality, which can bedevil other executives proud of their employer's past. He recalls:

The first thing which struck me when I came here was the way in which profits just leaked away. When I arrived in 1974 I saw the need for us to keep away from the chain stores battle, for it was forcing us into fringe lines and fringe activities, all of which were rather expensive and, as it seemed to me, the dominant struggle inside Debenhams was, initially, to do the things we needed to do well as a department store trader, and as inexpensively as possible. Companies with high overheads are the ones which go down the drain.

In this respect, we have experienced some success. Our cost structure is improving. When I came in, for example, our credit amounted to 15 per cent of the business but was costing £2½m a year in terms of lost interest and administrative charges. That was a very heavy burden. Now we have trebled the credit trade and it costs us nil, for we receive enough in interest to pay for the expenses of running a good credit system. So the incremental sales we obtain through credit terms are won for nothing.

The tendency in department stores will, if not watched, be towards a kind of indiscipline and slackness at every level. The problem is imposing discipline at various levels without destroying the urge to sell. There are strong salesmen in our various businesses and they need to be motivated. Central control can destroy something at individual store level, such as buying ability, but that is worthless unless replaced by something worthwhile in terms of the central control. If you like, the greatest feature in our struggle over the past decade or so has been about building up centralized control which clearly replaces the very good things which were taken away.

Thornton is ruthless in condemning what he calls the 'bumbling along at local level and the inefficiency of some stores', while recognizing that central buying has enlarged the scale of mistakes if some substantial purchasing commitment goes awry. The centralized structure for coordination of a big trading empire has to be kept lean to avoid building up layers of people over the individual stores. The scalpel must come out every three years or so.

Merchandising has to be a total commitment. Debenhams has to monitor the chain of supply right from production, through delivery, and down to the point of sale. Quality is not just about control of individual goods provided by suppliers but ensuring control is exercised at the point of sales. Marketing involves not just putting good lines before customers but also selling credit services. He explains:

I do not agonise at all over decisions. Take Browns of Chester, a fine store. I resisted the temptation to change the name to Debenhams as in the case of other stores. Browns at this stage is self-evidently a better name in Chester than Debenhams. Although this leads to complications in our promotional programmes – and remember there are half a dozen other stores with their original names – I am sure the good name of Debenhams will in the long run catch up and take over the good names of Browns and others. Then we will make the change. Customers anyway can see the Debenhams brand name on certain stock. We are firmly committed to use the Debenhams name and there is no question of going back on this.

I like department stores. Looking back on my earlier career, I realize that I left the world of chain stores because they began to bore me. I think there is little risk of this with department stores. The way we are now setting ourselves up and tending to diversify at the centre to increase the strength of buying groups is exciting. We are now endeavouring to create one-stop shopping centres where customers can get most things to satisfy customers for household goods, clothing, leisure or furnishing. Everyone – men, women, and children – are our customers.

The average British Home Stores is perhaps 20 000 square feet of sales space and Marks & Spencer say 30 000 square feet. Here in Debenhams the average is between 50 000 and 60 000 square feet of selling area per store. So we can do a wider range of selling, offering an ever changing kaleidoscopic merchandise. Remember a quarter of our trade is now on credit. It will be the lack of credit, when the trend is towards reduction in cash transactions, which will contain chains and supermarket operators to certain price levels. For example, I can sell with impunity a bed for £200. Banking cards are not nearly as flexible as our credit, and remember footage inhibits invasion of some types of our trade.

A big group such as Debenhams has roughly 5m square feet of selling space in town centres around Britain. In spite of much talk about out-of-town development, the trend is now towards urban renewal and refurbishing inner cities. Thornton is scornful of attacks on department stores as dying giants, especially when their share of retail trade has actually begun to expand again. He says:

We are not hesitating to build department stores with potential. These stores have a great future and tremendous potential for growth, too. That is why you will find rebuilding in progress everywhere, and conversions are often the same as a new store. It's happening everywhere – Croydon, Swansea, Cardiff, Stockport, Harrow, Reading, Ipswich, to name a selection. This is no contraction but a statement of our faith in putting something back into retailing. Historians will look back and say here were devotees of department stores, not butchers bent on destruction.

Mind you, it is easy to spend money, harder to make these stores pay. I am caught in a particularly horrid dilemma. We have very large stores and, although the staff costs and other costs are higher than the chains per pound of sales they are lower per square foot. I want to search out the revenues of the business and to raise them so can get the higher price per foot and a lower percentage of staff costs per pound of sales.

At the same time, in order to give the value I have got to reduce the staff costs so that our prices are competitive. We are down to an irreducible minimum on our sales floors in the sense that the department stores have got about 6000 full-time staff to cover 5m square feet. Marks & Spencer probably have 15 000 staff to cover 6m feet, so our efficiency per foot is much higher than theirs, but this leads to a parallel inefficiency in terms of what may appear to be poor service.

Put simply, income has to rise but we can only cut costs so far. In a way, more self-selection where customers do the work, and the use of stores within stores, such as Cresta, Windsmoor, English Lady, Hamleys and so on, assist too. We are able to call on Lotus to help in footwear and Caters to develop food hall expertise.

Thornton readily admits the customer can be easily confused by shops within shops – at least the unprepared customer. People are getting used to the practice as it is progressively expanded. Names such as Hardy Amies, Hamleys, and New Dimension are being brought into closer relationship with the parent group.

Where will Debenhams go in the next ten years? The chief executive sees the group moving up market ('what a nasty phrase') by using the credit tool. 'We will be on top of the pile,' he says without a hint of hesitation. A turnover of £1000m, and half the trade on credit should be attainable by the mid-1980s. He predicts:

Debenhams will be the dream shops by then. It will be the place to which people will gravitate for their more outlandish fantasies to be satisfied as well as other needs. There will be more casualties in retailing, and no doubt more and more department stores will sell out to people like us. Ahead I see a leisure world, not a sports world. Leisure homes, leisure furniture, leisure clothing, and leisure activities. I expect in ten years to take part in an extraordinary revolution with our stores looking quite different. This is our task, to reflect aspects of a changing life style. Looking even here in my office, who would have imagined this furniture and decor ten years back? People are throwing off their constraints and we can help them to express their fantasies in clothes, furnishing or whatever.

Thornton stops short of spelling out the future in great detail. Yet there is sufficient evidence to support his view of customers. In the sixties, the washing machine, refrigerator, TV set, and car became universal possessions. But with workshop kitchens and mobility, consumers remain unsatisfied. Even gleaming supermarkets no longer hold out excitement in shopping. Grocery buying has become a matter of pricing items of a similar kind and trusting to a store's quality control. The satisfaction in choice and selection gets lost at the check-out queue.

Consumers find in department stores and many chain stores places to roam, touch, and to try on clothes. Men have overcome decades of inhibition in dress and splash their faces with the latest toiletries. The TV set is just a fixture compared with the new high fidelity electrical goods. They buy power tools and fancy footwear, car rally jackets and wet suits. Children expect expensive toys, games, track suits, and other things. Babies are pampered with furniture and equipment. Women dress with both style and a disregard for past distinctions between young and old. They will spend £50 on fashion boots and £1 on a sale dress of indeterminate pedigree, but feel affronted if a can of food is a penny dearer in one shop compared with another.

Perhaps retailers need to attract more psychologists to their executive staff to supplement the accountants, salesmen, economists, and buyers. Debenhams' top management may engage in complicated sale and leaseback property deals and juggle with computerized figures but its people find it hardest to think of a short phrase to describe what they are about.

One who did not hesitate when asked was the chairman. Sir Anthony said instantly: 'People should *enjoy* shopping in department stores.' Shopping, he feels, can be a pleasure, and enjoyment is a condition of pleasure.

Burney is a friendly ambassador for the department stores he once only knew as a customer. He came to custodianship without any preconceived opinions, except those deriving from being a customer.

Enjoyment covers a multitude of possibilities. It is the merchandise, it's the value for money, it's good service, it's the delivery, the reliability and quality – all these sort of things can be wrapped up, as far as I am concerned, in the enjoyment of shopping at a Debenhams store. If there is a pleasant environment and an atmosphere of a willingness to please, people are in the right frame of mind for us to help them. Some of the niceties of the past have got to go because you really cannot afford to keep them. We used to have a very nice perfumery department, for example, down here in Wigmore Street and some charming saleswomen who had been there for ages and ages and their customers used to come in and sit there for hours: very nice and very pleasant, but what was sold surely did not justify this rather splendid service.

The carriage trade was lovely at its best, but now when you sell you must have a measure of impersonality when you have people milling round on crowded floors, picking up merchandise and prepared to carry it to a cash desk. This, I am afraid, has to be modern shopping. There is no getting away from it. Even my wife goes into a shop as seldom as possible because she thinks it is ghastly. We are trying to correct the balance by making shopping enjoyable within everyone's circumstances.

There was a lot of paternalism in a business like ours, if we look back. One of the nice things about the retail trade, you know, is that one argues that small is beautiful and something is lost when family businesses, which had a certain sense of responsibility towards their employees, are taken over. But even today one retains a special sense of communication within individual stores. Their size within a large group is perfect for a store director still to know everyone by name and really communicate. If you have a good store director, you have a good store. We can get a lot of advantages if we can solve the problems of communication about what we are doing and where we are going between those of us at the centre and those of our people dealing with sales staff and the public. We get too desk-bound. Perhaps our offices are much too comfortable. We should move all the furniture out and sit on the floor, and then we would see people going round a lot more than we do. It really is something special when those of us serving at the centre can get into the stores. Time, not desire, is what keeps too many of us away from our stores.

Debenhams has overhauled pensions and sorted out neglect of loyal staff. The system for recruiting new talent is being improved and a career structure spanning stores and general management has begun to emerge:

I have long fought a battle elsewhere on careers: the system whereby one becomes an accountant, for example, and always remains an accountant. In a business like this we can offer opportunities and it is wrong that retailing gets ignored say by undergraduates to schoolmasters advising on commercial opportunities.

I believe that training in a business like Debenhams is about as wide as one can get. There is finance, merchandise, selling, marketing, personnel – everything, from insights into manufacturing, buying, property, to general administration.

The Debenhams Group now comprises over seventy department stores and embraces numerous other diverse businesses, such as H. & M. Rayne, I. Miller in the United States, Hardy Amies, the Cavendish Medical Centre, and Greens Cameras. The absorption of Cresta, Caters, Hamleys, New Dimension and Lotus is contributing to an ever widening spread of activities whose success has to be measured by profits. In the mid-sixties, net profit before tax hovered around £6m. By 1977 it was over £18m. In ten years sales have risen by 300 per cent, no mean achievement and not due solely to acquisitions, for the organic turnover has risen markedly.

The past methods are not forgotten. At Harvey Nichols a local management is given fairly free range to handle what is known as the Knightsbridge trade, still considered something very special, meriting decentralized supervision. Money has been poured into refurbishing the Harvey Nichols business and its promotional activity belies any reluctance to try out new ideas on a lingering carriage trade which is increasingly backed by overseas visitors and the affluent meritocracy. The Marshall & Snelgrove and Woollands

178

Swan & Edgar survives with its original name

names may have gone, but Harvey Nichols and Swan and Edgar survive. Harrods flourishes, but Derry & Toms and Pontings have long gone from Kensington.

No different have been the fates of the Bobbys, Jones, Plummers, Browns, Kendal Milnes, Allders, Grants, Bentalls, and all the other names threaded into the fabric of British retailing, past and present. Across spans of years, various owners and managers have played out a game of Scrabble which can never finish so long as customers want departmentalized shopping. Excellence in storekeeping springs from history, but is maintained by the present and the future.

No one is forced to enter any given store, and a good name helps to attract our modern footloose consumer, with cheque book and credit card at the ready. What determines a good name from a bad one is what retailing is all about. Reputations are won, lost, and regained not by searching through archives or kindling memories to define excellence. It shines from any store which cares about customers, and is never guaranteed by the splendour of its surroundings or its history. A market trader and the grandest store director in a big city may represent two extremes in 'standing shop' yet each can excel against their particular rivals in a common endeavour – the mutual satisfaction of buyer and seller.

179

Appendix

Nostalgia is a pleasurable emotion and Britain, after more than thirty years at general peace with a world she once dominated, has tended to seek solace in her history and renowned traditions. Her greatness derived from many things, and the development of her institutions has tended to overshadow the enormous contribution to social progress of her distributive system which parallelled the industrial revolution.

Both small and large-scale enterprises had their origins in the dreams and ambitions of individuals. The story of British retailing is one of humble ventures by small shopkeepers. Commercial empires such as Debenhams are nothing but a conglomeration of their original endeavours, and, big and powerful as the group may appear, the individual store is still the only means by which the customer will judge a reputation. Nostalgia there may be for many of the lost names, dated modes, buildings, and personal service, but memories need to allow for the benefits of progress.

The impact of department stores on towns and cities has always been underrated. They were often at the heart of the communities they served and their names cause instant recognition among those who grew up with their services. One by one, however, the names vanish, and not even those who regret their passing can hope to persuade the young that there is a missing dimension in their lives. Shops which nourished fashion can never secure their future without concentrating on the young, who in turn will have their own memories to draw upon in evaluating the stores of their lifetimes.

One of the survivors is Harvey Nichols, which for more than fifty years has been in Debenhams' ownership. Founded in 1813 by Benjamin Harvey,

Harvey Nichols
Below: *Receipt for one quarter's rent, 1871*
Below right: *Bill envelope, 1863*

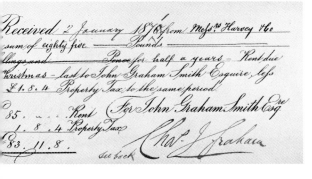

Harvey Nichols *The new building, 1900*

who opened a linen store in Lowndes Terrace, on the corner of London's Sloane Street, the business later prospered in premises known as Commerce House, under the title B. Harvey & Co. On his death, Benjamin Harvey willed the business to his daughter Elizabeth, but on the condition that she took the silk buyer, one Colonel Nichols, into partnership. Nichols's title is believed to have derived from his membership of the Volunteer Movement, formed against the possibility of an invasion of Britain by France.

Subsequently Harvey Nichols became one of the most fashionable retail houses in Knightsbridge, which had benefited from its proximity to the original Crystal Palace in Hyde Park. Linens and silks were the staple stock in trade, but later, furnishings, particularly carpets, became a speciality, too. Turkish and Indian carpets supplied by Harvey Nichols were much prized, and the advice of the Knightsbridge buyers was to be made available later to other Debenhams' stores.

Such was the store's reputation that, in the 1920s, casement fabrics, for example, could be sold at around 10s. and £1 per yard compared with 3d. to 4d. a yard at popular shops. At that time, an average married man's wage in the drapery trade was about £2 per week, and even this figure was higher than the average industrial wage. Today, old catalogues of goods sold by Harvey Nichols are collectors' items, monitoring as they do the art and design of fabrics, carpets and other lines through whole epochs.

Whereas Harvey Nichols survived, the name of Woolland Bros, which spanned that part of Knightsbridge opposite Albert Gate, has gone. Woollands overreached itself after building grand premises, and the owners tried to seek help from Debenhams. Magnificent billheads, which today can be found framed on the walls of some homes, were written out in pen and ink by clerks sitting on high stools at long desks. Gone, too, is the still renowned

ones of Bristol, c. 1908

name of Marshall & Snelgrove, which became no less familiar when in its heyday it spread across the North of England. Yet the stores of Britain's capital city cannot be allowed to overshadow those beyond the boundaries, for hundreds of great names in master storekeeping never aspired to London premises.

Two of the commonest names in Britain are Jones and Smith, so it is not surprising to find these names well represented in storekeeping. Edwin Jones and Co. of Southampton, a major department store and the first to fit an escalator in Southern England, became entwined with the quite separate Jones of Bristol. This came about through the financial manoeuvres of Clarence Hatry, whose Drapery Trust in the twenties acquired the famous Bon Marché of Gloucester from the Pope family, with a proviso that, in turn, the 'Bon' (as it was called in Debenhams) bought the Smith stores at Nuneaton, Stratford and Bedworth. During the negotiations, Hatry took over the two separate Jones enterprises, using money from one deal to fund another, and creating a paper chase in which one business paid dividends to another. For many years, one director of Jones at Southampton was paid commission on profits from Jones at Bristol, whose profits in turn were boosted by arrangements with the Bon Marché and Smith firms.

183

Relatively humble was Staddons, a popular store serving the thickly populated area of East London and offering keen prices along the Barking Road. Passers-by appreciated a large protruding street clock, which could be seen from three angles. Such clocks became commonplace. In the cathedral city of Canterbury grew the House of Lefevre, which later traded elsewhere in Kent. Lefevre became an important training ground for many future department store managers and was noted for its particularly happy staff, with a tradition of staging concert parties for their neighbourhood.

In the City of London once stood the great mantle, shawl and juvenile warehouse of D. Nicholson & Co., which developed a huge lunchtime trade with office and other City staff, though it was empty at most other times. Founded in 1843, the firm later became an outpost of the West End's Debenham & Freebody at St Paul's Churchyard. The name of Nicholson was to be transferred to a modern store at Bromley, Kent, which was developed on the site of a disused cinema.

East Anglia has long boasted great names in departmental trading. One of the greatest was Footmans, founded by Robert Footman in 1815 in the Buttermarket at Ipswich, and subsequently developing several branch stores. Footman's Waterloo House, erected in 1842, was among the most impressive shop buildings in Britain. Footman later entered into partnership with William Pretty, and a civic dignitary, Alderman A. F. Nicolson. Footmans gained a big reputation for furnishings, and pioneered a horse-drawn removal business, paper-hangings ('2000 pieces to choose from'), and the sale of prams ('800 always in stock'). It was among the earliest retailers of sewing machines, and entered the corset manufacturing business in the mid-nineteenth century.

Another great East Anglian name was Curls, of Norwich, formed by three brothers Edward, Jacob and Henley around 1860 at the corner of St Stephen Street. In 1902 Curls built a major new store with a long window frontage lit by eleven Ediswan lamps, each of 200 candlepower. The shop had a massive domed glass roof. East Anglia was to be peppered with names no less prestigious in shopkeeping, such as Chamberlins, Buntings, Bonds, and Garlands, and became a breeding ground of many top managers of stores around Britain. A great store which did not carry the founder's name was Bon Marché. J. R. Pope founded the Bon Marché Drapery Company at Northgate Street in 1889. One of his sons, Frederick J. Pope, was trained in London and another, George A. Pope, learned drapery in Exeter and Oxford. Frederick and George in due course turned a relatively modest enterprise into a huge store. Its founder was commemorated with a huge clock high above the corner of the premises, which attracted many visiting storekeepers from all parts of the country. Like so many provincial department stores, Bon Marché became a social rendezvous. Its 500-seat restaurant was the very heart of Gloucester's society in the twenties and thirties.

More than a few department storekeepers became pillars of their communities. The founder of Bon Marché became the city's High Sheriff and Edwin Jones, a thwarted Liberal Parliamentary candidate, became Mayor of Southampton.

By 1933, Edwin Jones of Southampton was one of the finest stores in

Spooners' 20 cwt Morris commercial van, built in 1925

England, a turreted fortress topped by a central clock tower from which it flew flags. The entrance was along a 300-foot arcade. This was shopkeeping at its best, for within was every conceivable service, from coal deliveries to one of the grandest food halls, equipped with butter packing and tea blending machines. There was hairdressing, a large travel bureau, a greengrocery (drawing on the shop's own farm), and a huge wholesale warehouse for supplying other Southern traders. Teams of cobblers worked out of sight on boot and shoe repairing, and footwear was sold in great quantity (Jones' expertise was later to be widely used by other Debenhams stores).

The competition among the stores was intense, in spite of their seemingly unhurried styles of management. Joseph Spooner, in 1858, opened a little draper's shop in Bedford Street, Plymouth, a road also selected by one John Yeo (twice Mayor of Plymouth) for a 'cash only' venture. Spooners pioneered motorized deliveries to their customers and created a reputation for complete house furnishing. Spooners never stopped expanding, and its great central store dominated all around until it was destroyed by enemy bombing in the Second World War. Yeo and Spooner stores were to be linked by a bridge when rebuilt after the war.

Most shops built reputations on some original feature of the founding firm. A. J. Soper opened his premises at the Promenade, Greenhill at Harrow-on-the-Hill as late as 1914, offering 'fancy drapery'. By 1922 Soper's merged with Green & Edwards, who ran a long established fashion business at Hampstead. Soper's name was restored in 1941, over a recently redeveloped store, with lifts, and a restaurant complete with resident pianist, cellist and violinist. Soper's were among the first stores to offer 'ready exchange of goods, or cash refunds' without arguments. Many of the pre-war housing estates in the area (a four-bedroomed house could be bought for

£350) were furnished by Soper's with items such as oak bedroom suites priced in 1938 at £11 19s. 6d., or twelve monthly payments of 20s. 6d.

Thomas Jones, who built showrooms at Wine Street, Bristol in 1843 (the year when Isambard Kingdom Brunel's ironship ss *Great Britain* was launched from the local shipyards) was one of the great innovators in window display. An exhibition of live Welsh ponies in the Jones windows prompted an unsuccessful legal action by Bristol Council. Jones marked the occasion by adopting the Council's coat of arms for his business, embellishing it with Welsh troops and a pony attacking the coat of arms.

The pioneers in department stores were a varied bunch. A farmer's boy, J. C. Smith, for example, in 1870 borrowed £500 from his newly wedded wife and set up in Wood Street, Stratford-upon-Avon. He lived over the shop and produced six children, establishing a long line of trading Smiths. His store featured displays of stock outside, along the pavement, to create an atmosphere of low-cost street trading. Every day assistants would hang up clothing and other goods onto rows of hooks screwed into the shopfront. Several assistants lived in, and slept under counters inside the cramped store. As business grew, branch stores opened and deliveries were made by hand carts and specially made cycle carts. Smiths were initiators of 'buyers bargain events'. There was even a silver cup to be awarded to the buyer offering the best bargains, upon which customers were invited to vote. Advertisements showed the buyers' names plus statements of their policies, simulating election addresses.

One of the most expansionist firms was Bobby & Co., founded in 1887 by Frederick J. Bobby at Margate, but greatly expanded by his sons Arthur and Herbert. As it grew in the South, so did the rival Plummers, and they traded against each other along the South Coast of England. Bobbys built many great stores, and bought Green & Son of Exeter which had particularly splendid showrooms and trading floors which matched those of London's great stores. At Exeter, rows of women would sit by long counters in the cloth, silk and serge departments, as frock-coated assistants paraded with their wares.

The personal fate of department store people was varied. William Plummer (whose name is enshrined in Plummer Roddis) drowned when the ss *Stella* was wrecked in the English Channel in 1899. A member of the Plymouth Brethren, he had founded a business in Hastings and at the time of his death had expanded into several south coast towns as far west as Bournemouth. Plummers became a major name in department stores. They manufactured upholstery and bought the first steam-engined lorries to carry large loads.

Slogans were popular among storekeepers. They were used on handbills, on hoardings, and in advertisements. Pauldens at All Saints, Manchester, greeted the arrival of motorized transport by adopting the slogan on all sales literature, 'Well Worth A Bus Ride.' William Paulden, the founder, was a farmer's son who defied all advice and opened his original shop in 1865 in a poor area along the Stretford Road. He was, however, convinced that trade could be built upon the earnings of the working classes around Manchester, and he offered good strong furniture at cheap prices, and hard wearing linoleums. Indeed, in linoleum, Pauldens became a noted name and heavily promoted its use when carpets were well beyond most families' means.

Pauldens were the first Manchester shop to use electric lighting after the founder bought the entire lighting equipment used for the Manchester Jubilee Exhibition in 1887. Later, many Manchester people saw their first moving pictures when Pauldens showed free films in its shop windows. The founder met a tragic death in an accident at Piccadilly railway station, and Pauldens was run for some years by his widow with as much enterprise as Elizabeth Harvey in Knightsbridge.

Not every founder of a department store had a guarantee of growth and survival. The Great Yarmouth concern, Arnolds, formed in 1869, had reached the verge of bankruptcy by the time Debenhams saved it from massive debts in 1936. The man who saved the store was John Bedford, later chairman of Debenhams, who subsequently handed it over to Fred Besley, later Debenhams' managing director.

Arnolds was an example of a store well integrated into the community, for in the Second World War the basement became an emergency hospital while trade continued on the ground floor above. Others provided ballrooms and restaurants for every kind of function, from wedding breakfasts to formal banquets. Often rooms were provided for societies or clubs, including local chambers of trade.

Stores were fascinating places, but few customers saw behind the scenes. Busbys of Bradford was a veritable hive of enterprise behind its mock Gothic elevation. The Yorkshire store installed a huge steam turbine to power a laundry, and there were great bakery ovens. One of England's first car valeting services was provided for motorized customers.

Most shops grew out of very rudimentary buildings. Early pictures of Stones of Romford, Essex, founded in 1864, resemble a frontier town of the Old West. Later there came a purpose-built store offering costumier and outfitting services, then a 4½-acre functional building replaced the lot in 1963. A typical example of how a series of disjointed premises could be

Stones of Romford

redeveloped was Tuttles, at Lowestoft in Suffolk, though the trade proved disappointing for some years after redevelopment by Debenhams.

The spread of electricity owes much to decisions by shopkeepers to replace gas lighting, providing examples of the merits in town centres for inspection by others. In the West Country, W. & A. Chapman, of Taunton, set up by two brothers from London in 1864, introduced electric illumination to the town. Chapman was a typical innovator, and some of the earliest Model-T Ford delivery vans were first seen struggling along the then poor roads of Somerset.

There is no doubt that department stores dominated town centres from Victorian times. Towns were proud of their central premises and civic authorities often actively assisted in their further expansion as trade boomed. A typical example among hundreds was Bonds at Chelmsford, where a series of developments are recorded on the same basic site from 1857 onwards. Bonds was an early pioneer of the practice of building long arcades of island windows as their main frontage, through which people could walk and take shelter as well as make preliminary inspections of window displays before entering the store.

One of the examples of how a store rooted itself in the heart of its city was Thornton-Varley at Kingston-upon-Hull. This grew out of a tiny shop started by Richard Thornton in 1870 and, as the business became grander, added not just to his property but also to his name, tacking on Varley. The business suffered from heavy bombing and moved around the city in a struggle for survival, until Debenhams rebuilt it on the original site.

One of the greatest hazards faced by earliest stores was fire. Insurance companies always rated them as prone to risks, and their records show scores of fires before the introduction of sprinklers and other devices of a preventive character. John Hubbard stood watching, helpless and crying, when the store he had built at South Street, Worthing, was destroyed in 1947. Rebuilding took four years. Fire ravaged Jermyn & Sons at Kings Lynn, Norfolk (drapers and furnishers to H.M. Queen Elizabeth II) in 1884 at the height of its Christmas trade. Everything was lost within an hour. Unabashed, the founder, Sir Alfred Jermyn started again, and from the ashes arose Jermyn & Perry and Jermyn & Scott, twin businesses trading side by side from one great building by 1890. Jermyn boasted in print that there was 'no such emporium within a radius of 40 miles' and called the store the 'Whiteleys' of the district.

Many early traders began as partnerships, which gave rise to a variety of names over the decades. In Nottingham, two young men, William Griffin and John Spalding, newly arrived from London, joined a local enterprise called Dickinson & Fazakerly, founded in 1846. The association was to give Nottingham a magnificent store, surrounding the City's famed Mikado café. Griffin & Spalding, as the business became known, were skilled caterers and on the staff were many skilled people, such as cabinet-makers and wood fitters. The firm furnished more than a few cinemas with those huge stage curtains so familiar to patrons of the Odeons, Granadas, and other cinemas whose buildings could be as grand and ornate as the big stores.

It was the habit of customers to shorten many names. Style & Gerrish at

The Romford store ablaze

Salisbury, founded in 1803 and built out from the original Saracens Head Inn, was always known as Styles, a useful name for a fashion trader. Nonetheless, Styles undertook many services, including funerals. The store owned at one time just one hearse and one 15 cwt delivery van. Once the hearse caught fire and the coffin it was carrying to a burial ceremony had to be removed to the grass verge until the 15 cwt van was summoned.

Among several stores as old as Debenhams was E. P. Rose at Bedford. Roses derived from a bow-fronted drapery shop set up in 1791. Pendleburys of Wigan traced its history back to Michael Milligan's little shop opened in 1780 at Standishgate, nearly 100 years before John Pendlebury acquired the enterprise and built his Crawford House (destroyed by fire in 1953).

Stores usually began as one shop, which acquired neighbouring premises. This tended to give them a rambling, often intriguing, atmosphere. One such store was that of Adnitt Brothers at Northampton, which included an old farmhouse in its early buildings with a splendid oak Jacobean staircase which everyone enjoyed ascending.

Some of the finest billheads and trade cards to be printed are those of Elliston & Cavell, founded at Magdalen Street, Oxford, in 1820 and among the first provincial stores to build gas-lit showrooms (the idea actually com-

189

ing from a Gravesend hosier and glover called Harry Rose, who bought the business in 1887).

Each store had its specialities. Noted as credit drapers were Affleck & Brown of Manchester, but it was the stock of dress fabrics which turned the premises into a haunt for early home dressmakers buying the first sewing machines. Lancashire folk knew their cloth, so it says much for Affleck & Brown's selection that they developed such a reputation.

In any roll-call of the great names in Northern storekeeping there will be a place for Matthias Robinson, which sprang out of West Hartlepool in 1875 and where the founder built his impressive Manchester House and what he called the Coliseum. The business moved into Leeds and Stockton-on-Tees. At Stockton, another Coliseum introduced one of the first Lamson pneumatic tubes for the cash collection system. The Leeds store of considerable proportions arose in Briggate, where a hotel was demolished along with a string of small shops. When the exterior of ornate stonework and Edwardian murals was cleaned up in 1971, the Leeds Civic Trust made an award for this 'building of outstanding interest'.

One example of a modern functional department store has to be Pauldens (now Debenhams) in Sheffield, offering 214 000 square feet of space and opened in 1965. Curiously, trading results were disappointing for some years, in spite of the design and utility of its fittings. This was not the case with a closely planned store opened at Harrow by Debenhams and embracing new concepts in floor planning to maximize trade on the available space.

The expansion of early department stores was not always secured by rebuilding on a large scale. Often branch businesses were spawned. Such was the case with Edward Greey, of Birmingham, who started as a small fancy draper in 1891. Of course, Greys built itself a flagship, in 1926, in the city centre, but its branch businesses are still remembered, especially for their straw hats, feathers and felts.

Department stores have a long association with the food trades, even if they were preoccupied with the fashion trades. Catering has always been associated with both large and small stores. Provisioning through a food hall on the ground floor of a department store, often with a separate entrance, has a long history. With their bacon slicers and delicatessens, these halls were often equipped with counters made from slabs of marble and had great atmosphere. Regular deliveries of weekly orders were abandoned with the advent of supermarkets.

Debenhams' stores have had many food halls, but in 1972 the group took over Cater Bros., founded in 1883 by Henry John Cater, a father of six children, in Roman Road, Bow, in London's East End. Caters had been specialists in fresh provisions, particularly bacons and teas. By 1939, Caters had twenty-six stores around London and were to be among the pioneers of the self-service system of selling groceries, leading on to the development of some of the first supermarkets.

The acquisition of businesses outside department stores has formed part of their traditional role of widening services. For its part, Debenhams now owns shops as historic as Hamleys, the toy firm which began as Noah's Ark in High Holborn in 1761 and moved to Regent Street in 1906, and as modern as Greens Camera shops or the fashion designers Hardy Amies. Names such as Raynes and Lotus in footwear may not be of equal age, but each has a considerable story.

But, even as a combination such as Debenhams diversifies and brings new and old names within its own premises as shops-within-shops, the world of department stores still prizes hundreds of names with a lineage as intriguing, as, for example, Browns of Chester. Browns began when a Miss Susannah Towsey of that city sent a buyer by six-day stage coach to London to buy fancy ribbons for her friends. In 1791 she married the local druggist, John Brown, and promptly set up shop in Eastgate Row. Generations have shopped at the original Georgian building to which was added a Victorian facade and pseudo-Gothic embellishments. The Brown family severed links with the store in 1908, but their name lives on until the people of Chester and Debenhams decide to take it down.

Stores owed their individual character to the people who worked within. Reputations, gained or lost, for service and selection of stock came from thousands upon thousands of men and women who went into trade. Their devotion and pride came from each other, whether dressing windows or tirelessly ignoring sore feet on the sales floor in the daily traffic of customers. Their names are not enshrined above shop facades, but they gave lifetimes to perpetuating the names of others.

It is small compensation to select just two, one a worker who just left his initials, and another his full name, in attempting to set down in the humblest of poetry some of their thoughts:

Just a Window Dresser

I open my eyes, I stretch and I yawn,
That's how I always greet the dawn.
And as out of the window I wearily gaze,
I think of the windows at shop in a daze,
And with awful effort I get out of bed,

Eight o'clock, and I feel half dead.
I shave and wash in a dreadful scurry,
Eat breakfast and leave in a terrible hurry
With cigarette, and first rays of sun
The day has only just begun.
I start at a trot and end with a run,
For I've got to clock in, and so much to be done.
Having said 'good morning' the hundredth time,
I start with gowns, pale pink and lime.
For this a setting must be sought,
An Axminster rug? A happy thought.
The rug in place, the stands all dressed,
An easy start, I am well blessed.
Then, after an hour, fixing buttons and straps,
Outside, on the glass, an old lady taps.
I go outside, not taking long,
'Young man,' says she, 'There's something wrong,
Just look at that model, she is a sight,
Her right arm's left, and her left arm right.'
Having thanked the old lady, I think you old terror,
I leave the old dear, convulsed at the error.
The model now normal and time for lunch,
I visit the café; talk, drink and munch.
Back again on the windows so well dressed,
A small girl's nose to a pane is pressed,
'That doll is queer, just look at it mummy,
It's five-and-six and showing its tummy.'
But alas, just then, an awful smash,
The hosiery window's gone in with a crash.
With the manager wearing an awful expression,
I sense there's going to be a depression;
And as the echo still resounds,
He says 'That's going to cost a few pounds.'
Porters arrive to clear up the mess,
I feel like taking the train to Loch Ness,
But instead to the studio I go,
There to look at the models, all in a row.
Some look lovely and some like tripe,
One has my lid on and holding my pipe.
Though a window-dresser I have no regrets,
I can carry baskets and put on corsets.
This sort of thing goes on every day,
And always on Fridays I want my pay,
But there's just one thing I don't think fair,
That is to leave a model bare.

R.C.
(*Bobby & Co. Ltd, Exeter*)

Daniel Dingle and You

My name is Daniel Dingle,
　　At least that's what we'll say,
Though it doesn't really matter,
　　Any rate until Pay Day.

I work with crowds of others
　　In a Departmental Store,
And like the rest of Drapers,
　　I suppose you'd say I'm poor.

Now don't think I'm a nuisance,
　　But I think its time I spoke,
As the number of complaints I hear
　　Is getting past a joke.

　　It seems that most Sales People,
　　Need to find out where they stand;
In relation to the other folk,
　　Who form our Selling Band.

It really is annoying
　　For the customer, you see,
To be sent down to the Basement
　　When she should have come to me.

If asking for the UNDERwear
　　You send her to the Shoes,
It's apt to make her angry,
　　And I'm sure it must confuse.

I think we'll start some classes,
　　To find out where you are,
In case you're asked for Linen Sheets,
Or for the Toy Bazaar.

You'd learn just where departments are,
　　The best way there as well,
And most important thing of all,
　　Exactly what they sell.

The next time that they ask you
　　'Where can I find So-and-So,'
Don't send them on a wild goose chase,
　　But tell them where to go.

Oliver Rapier
(*Plummers, Hastings*.) *May 1937*

Index